TEEN VICTIMS
of the
NAZI REGIME

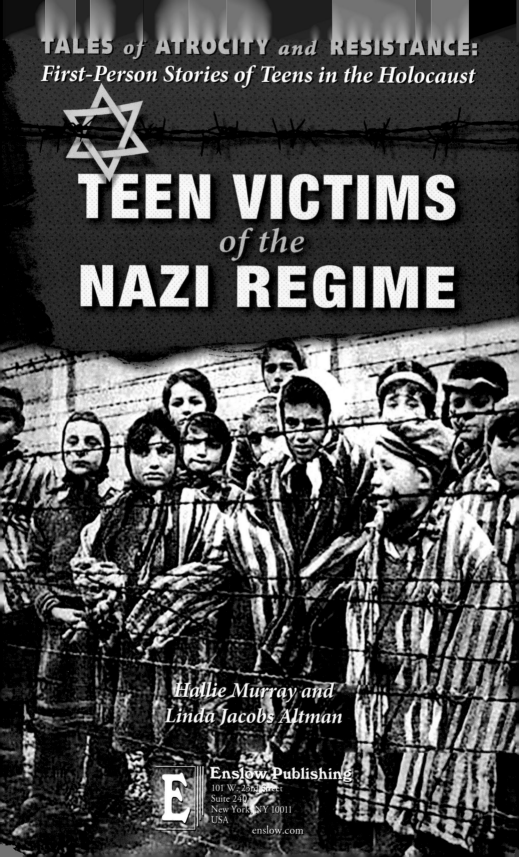

TALES *of* ATROCITY *and* RESISTANCE:
First-Person Stories of Teens in the Holocaust

TEEN VICTIMS
of the
NAZI REGIME

*Hallie Murray and
Linda Jacobs Altman*

Enslow Publishing
101 W. 23rd Street
Suite 240
New York, NY 10011
USA
enslow.com

Special thanks to the people of the United States Holocaust Memorial Museum in Washington, DC, for all their help in completing this book.

Published in 2019 by Enslow Publishing, LLC.
101 W. 23rd Street, Suite 240, New York, NY 10011

Library of Congress Cataloging-in-Publication Data

Names: Murray, Hallie. | Altman, Linda Jacobs.
Title: Teen victims of the Nazi regime / Hallie Murray and Linda Jacobs Altman.
Description: New York : Enslow Publishing, 2019. | Series: Tales of atrocity and resistance: first-person stories of teens in the holocaust | Includes bibliographic references and index.
Identifiers: LCCN 2018001169 | ISBN 9780766098404 (pbk.) | ISBN 9780766098398 (library bound)
Subjects: LCSH: Holocaust, Jewish (1939–1945)—Juvenile literature.| Jews—Persecutions—Germany—Juvenile literature. | Jewish children in the Holocaust—Juvenile literature. | Germany—Ethnic relations—Juvenile literature.
Classification: LCC D804.34 M87 2019 | DDC 940.53/40835—dc23
LC record available at https://lccn.loc.gov/2018001169

Printed in the United States of America

Portions of this book originally appeared in *Shattered Youth in Nazi Germany* by Linda Jacobs Altman.

To Our Readers: We have done our best to make sure all website addresses in this book were active and appropriate when we went to press. However, the author and the publisher have no control over and assume no liability for the material available on those websites or on any websites they may link to. Any comments or suggestions can be sent by e-mail to customerservice@enslow.com.

Photo Credits: Cover, pp. 3, 34–35 Keystone/Hulton Archive/Getty Images; pp. 8–9 Central Press/Picture Post/Getty Images; pp. 13, 46, 86–87 Hulton Deutsch/Corbis Historical/Getty Images; pp. 16–17, 36, 96–97, 100–101 ullstein bild/Getty Images; pp. 22–23 Hulton Archive/Getty Images; pp. 26–27 Roger Viollet/Getty Images; p. 30 John Frost Newspapers/Alamy Stock Photo; pp. 40–41, 66 Keystone-France/Gamma-Keystone/Getty Images; pp. 50–51 Bettmann/Getty Images; pp. 56–57 Mondadori Portfolio/Getty Images; p. 58 FALKENSTEINFOTO/Alamy Stock Photo; pp. 61, 90–91, 94–95, 104 Universal History Archive/Universal Images Group/Getty Images; pp. 63, 73, 112 Universal Images Group/Getty Images; p. 71 Corbis Historical/Getty Images; pp. 76–77 United States Holocaust Memorial Museum, courtesy of Waltraud & Annemarie Kusserow; pp. 80–81 United States Holocaust Memorial Museum, courtesy of Jerzy Ficowski; p. 107 Authenticated News/Archive Photos/Getty Images; p. 111 Hulton Archive/Archive Photos/Getty Images; pp. 114–115 Galerie Bilderwelt/Hulton Archive/Getty Images; cover and interior pages graphic elements kikujungboy/Shutterstock .com (barbed wire), ghenadie/Shutterstock.com (Star of David).

Contents

Introduction

Hatred and prejudice thrive in times of fear. The aftermath of World War I was one such time: the war had decimated Germany's economy, and German citizens were incredibly scared and angry, and many people wanted someone to blame for the lack of jobs and their loss in the war. Although anti-Semitism has always existed in Europe, some people seized on the false idea that Jewish Germans had betrayed their country and contributed to the loss. It was amid this heightened anti-Semitism that the Nazi Party gained power. At first just a fringe group, soon Nazis were represented throughout the German government.

After Adolf Hitler gained complete control over Germany in 1934, Nazi ideas became more and more prevalent throughout German thought and culture. Anti-Semitic beliefs were made to seem like the norm, and Nazis created vast amounts of propaganda in order to stoke hatred against Jews in Germany. In autumn of 1938, a Jewish teenager in Paris unwittingly gave Nazi propagandists exactly what they wanted—an event they could use to justify extreme cruelty against and mass murder of Jews in Nazi Germany.

Herschel Grynszpan was seventeen years old when he was arrested in Paris after shooting Ernst vom Rath. His eventual fate is unknown, but he likely died in a camp within the year.

On November 7, 1938, seventeen-year-old Herschel Grynszpan walked into the German embassy in Paris and asked to speak to an official. When the receptionist asked the nature of his business, Grynszpan would only say that it was urgent and of a personal nature. The clerk directed him to Ernst vom Rath, the only attaché available at the time. Once inside vom Rath's office, Grynszpan took out a gun and fired at point-blank range, grievously wounding vom Rath.

Grynszpan declared that he had acted "in the name of 12,000 persecuted Jews."[1] Those Jews were Polish citizens who had been living in Germany, some for many years, hoping that things would improve. They hadn't. In October 1938, Nazi troops snatched Jews from their homes, packed them into trains like so much cargo, and dumped them at the Polish border. In this wasteland between two nations, there was never enough food to go around. They lived in makeshift dwellings, without decent sanitary facilities. Worse yet, there seemed to be no end to their suffering. Germany would not take them back, and Poland would not let them in. Herschel Grynszpan's family was among these trapped Jews, and he had shot vom Rath out of desperation and anger at their plight.

While Ernst vom Rath fought for his life in a Paris hospital, the headline of every German newspaper screamed the news: a German diplomat had been shot by a Jewish assassin. The stories appeared on the morning of November 8. By that evening, angry Germans roamed the streets, harassing every Jew they could find. The Nazi propaganda chief, Joseph Goebbels, exploited this anger, using every available resource to whip up strong anti-Jewish feelings. By November 9, the anger was almost palpable, and Reinhard Heydrich, the "blond beast" as he was often called, stepped into the picture

On November 9, mobs raged through German cities and towns, setting fire to synagogues, smashing windows, destroying Jewish property, and brutalizing Jewish people. The rioting was meant to appear completely spontaneous, though in fact it was planned. After that night, the shattered glass of shop windows lay in mounds on the sidewalks, hence the name Kristallnacht, or the Night of Broken Glass. According to Heydrich, the violence of November 9 and 10 left 7,500 businesses destroyed, saw 267 synagogues burned to the ground, and resulted in the deaths of 92 Jews.[2]

After the horror and violence of Kristallnacht, the Nazis had about 25,000 Jewish men arrested and then sent them to concentration camps. Most were released about two weeks later, but the Nazis had made their point: the

Jewish community as a whole would be punished for the acts of one member.

Herschel Grynszpan faded from public view along with headlines about the assassination and was probably executed quietly, soon after his transfer to Germany. But his actions have had a lasting legacy. Many historians trace the beginning of the Holocaust back to Kristallnacht. Using the act of a desperate teenager as an excuse, the Nazis launched nationwide violence against the Jews. Burning synagogues and smashed windows stunned the world, terrified Jewish communities, and previewed the murderous fury that would soon descend on the Jews of Europe.

Chapter 1

Institutional Anti-Semitism

Although Germany's Nazi era began on January 30, 1933, when President Paul von Hindenburg appointed Adolf Hitler to the office of chancellor, the Nazi Party had already existed for over a decade before Hitler came to power. The Nazi Party was started in 1920 as a nationalist group that was politically against communism. Made up of people who had fought against communism in Germany after World War I, the Nazi Party based its political philosophy on extreme nationalism, racism, and authoritarianism. Nazis wanted to create a unified German state that was "racially pure" and free of people like Jews, Romani, political dissidents, and those with physical disabilities in order to become great.

Hitler's Ascent to Power

For most of the time that the German Nazi Party was active—1920 to 1945—Adolf Hitler was its leader. Hitler was a high school dropout with a spotty work record, but he knew how to sway the masses. With rallies, parades, and fiery speeches, he transformed the Nazi Party from an unknown extremist group into a national force. The term "Nazi" is a nickname, drawn from the first word of the party's full name: National Socialist German Workers' Party.

Hitler was a powerful speaker. He promised a glorious future in which a German "master race" would forge the greatest empire the world had ever seen. War was the price of building that empire. Genocide—the systematic killing of entire racial, cultural, or religious groups—was the price of perfecting the "Aryan" race, which is what Hitler called the Germanic and Nordic peoples.

Hitler's unique speech patterns and passionate delivery made him a very powerful speaker. Many people shared his reprehensible beliefs, but he became a famous figure who represented the Nazi Party both in Germany and abroad.

13

President von Hindenburg neither liked nor trusted Hitler. He considered Hitler little more than a thug with a knack for rabble-rousing.[1] But the president's advisors thought differently. They advisors knew about Hitler's extremism, but they thought they could control him. Let Hitler be the public face of government, they said. Let him rally the masses with his pomp and pageantry. But behind the scenes, vice chancellor Franz von Papen would be in charge.

The advisors soon realized they had made a terrible mistake. Nobody could control Hitler. From the first moment he became chancellor, he began transforming Germany into a Nazi state and governed Nazi Germany as an all-powerful dictator whose smallest word had the force of law.

Celebrating Hitler's Appointment

On the night Hitler was appointed chancellor, Nazis throughout Germany celebrated with torchlight parades. In the capital city of Berlin, thousands of brown-uniformed storm troopers, as the Nazi militiamen were often called, marched past the chancellery. Hitler stood on the balcony, taking their stiff-armed Nazi salute.

For gentile, or non-Jewish, teenager Melita Maschmann, the procession was a life-changing event. More than thirty years later, she wrote that

> some of the uncanny feel of that night remains with me even today. The crashing tread of the feet, the somber pomp of the red and black flags, the flickering light from the torches on the faces and the songs with melodies that were at once aggressive and sentimental.

For hours the columns marched by . . . I longed
to hurl myself into this current, to be submerged and
borne along by it . . . At one point somebody suddenly
leaped from the ranks of the marchers and struck a man
who had been standing only a few paces away from us.
Perhaps he had made a hostile remark. I saw him fall
to the ground with blood streaming down his face and
I heard him cry out . . . The image of him haunted me
for days.

The horror it inspired in me was . . . spiced with an
intoxicating joy. "For the flag we are ready to die," the
torchbearers had sung.[2]

For Melita Maschmann, joy won out over horror. She
went on to become a loyal Nazi and a leader in the League
of German Girls, or Bund Deutscher Mädchen (BDM).

That same night, a rabbi's son in the town of Gross-
Strehlitz ended up marching in a torchlight parade. Ezra
BenGershôm was eleven years old when his class was
invited to take part in a huge community celebration:

When I arrived at school . . . the pupils were already
formed up in columns, class by class, and were preparing
to march through the town behind their teachers. I
quickly got into line and, like all the others, had a torch
thrust into my hand.

I was not sure what we were celebrating . . . I was 11
years old and it gave me enormous pleasure not to be
an onlooker for once but actually to be taking part in
the procession . . . [They] were even letting us march in
step behind a military band, holding blazing torches in
our hands.

As we reached the more brightly lit streets of the
town centre, I noticed that the procession included
. . . Hitler Youth and SA [storm trooper] detachments.

These members of the League of German Girls, the Nazi organization for girls ages ten to eighteen, are wearing shirts with the organization's symbol, a black swastika on a red and white checked diamond.

The "military band" turned out to be a regular SA formation. What was going on? . . . It was not until long after that memorable evening that I realized the truth: our torchlight procession had been to celebrate Hitler's appointment as chancellor.[3]

The Racist Pursuit of "Perfection"

Racism and anti-Semitism, or hatred of Jews, were part of Nazism from the very beginning. The Nazis considered Poles, Russians, and Gypsies "subhuman" and made it their mission to murder people whom they viewed as undeserving of life. They also killed infants with birth defects, people with mental illness or developmental issues, and those who had simply grown too old to be considered "useful" in the new Germany.

In addition to killing these people, the Nazis sterilized thousands, often without their knowledge or consent. They wanted to be sure that people with genetic defects could not have children. Of course, Nazism relied heavily on racist biological ideas, and Nazis considered being "racially inferior" a genetic defect. The Nazis, led by Hitler, envisioned a new world order where Germany, expanded beyond its current borders, would be the home of a "master race" of "Aryans," Germans of Nordic ancestry who were useful to the state and supported Hitler's racist, nationalist ideology.

Nazis also sterilized many people whose only "defect" was having part-African ancestry. Mixed-race children faced a hard life in Hitler's Germany. Hans Massaquoi experienced these hardships firsthand. A son of a German mother and an African father, Hans was only seven years old when Hitler came to power. At first, Hans celebrated with his friends. Not until a year later did he realize the danger he was in:

> Once Hitler was firmly in control of the nation, there . . . was never a dull moment in Hamburg. Each week brought new major events and excitement . . . There were endless processions of SS, SA, and Hitler Youth units marching through the city to . . . the fighting marches of the Nazi movement, dramatic torchlight parades at night, and fireworks over the [lake]. None of these events . . . [seemed to present] any . . . personal threat until the . . . early part of 1934, when I was in the third grade. On that particular day . . . I got my first inkling of the danger the Nazi regime might pose for me.
>
> It was a bizarre twist of fate that the newly formed local Nazi chapter chose for its weekly meeting place Zanoletti's tavern and meeting hall, [next] to the apartment building in which we lived. For several months, our new neighbors and I were oblivious to each other's existence . . . Then the inevitable occurred. It happened on a beautiful spring Sunday that had started . . . with a [Nazi] parade through our neighborhood . . . [It] . . . had attracted large crowds of spectators, who were lining the parade route . . . I watched until the last unit of storm troopers had marched by and the crowd started to disperse.
>
> As I walked home, I heard loud singing and shouting coming from the building next to ours . . . I tried to catch a glimpse through the wide open door of Zanoletti's meeting hall. It was packed [with] . . . brownshirts . . . None of them seemed to notice me. . . . Or so I thought. Suddenly, I felt myself grabbed from behind by two

huge fists and lifted into the air . . . I stretched and bent . . . like a fish on a hook. The next thing I knew, I had slipped from the grip of the two fists and was running as fast as I could . . . I might have made good my escape had it not been for two other Brownshirts who . . . blocked my path. Like a hawk descending on his prey, the SA trooper reclaimed his hapless quarry and this time, none of my kicking, wiggling, and biting could loosen his viselike grip . . . The SA trooper was about to lift me to the speaker's platform, apparently as an exhibit of . . . racial defilement when he found himself confronted by an enraged woman who was staring at him with hate-filled eyes . . . Momentarily startled by this trembling, yet apparently fearless woman, the giant SA trooper loosened his grip. Before . . . anyone . . . could comprehend what was taking place, I was once again snatched and dragged through the carousing throng, but this time by my mother, who hauled me off to the relative safety of our home.[4]

Germany Becomes Hostile to Jews

Of all the targeted groups, Hitler reserved his deepest hatred for the Jews. He said they were like vermin and called upon good Germans to make their country, and eventually all of Europe, *Judenfrei*, or free of Jews. As Nazis gained increasing control of Germany's government, they worked to strip German Jews of their livelihood, their citizenship, and even their right to live. Later they did the same to Jews in the countries they occupied during the war.

The first measures taken against Jews focused on depriving them of work and financial freedom. The official persecution of Jews began with a one-day boycott

Storm Troopers: Specialist Soldiers and Nazi Protectors

When someone says "storm troopers," the first thing most Americans think of is probably *Star Wars*, not Nazis, but storm troopers were a serious fighting unit in the German and Nazi military. In World War I, the word "storm trooper" referred to a specialized member of the German military. After Hitler rose to power, the term was used to refer to members of the militarized branch of the Nazi Party. Storm troopers, also known as brownshirts or SA troops, fought against other parties and provided protection for Nazi leaders and Nazi gatherings. Storm troopers lost power in 1934, and their role was quickly usurped by the Schutzstaffel, the SS.

of Jewish businesses on April 1, 1933. Uniformed storm troopers stood outside of Jewish businesses, telling people not to go inside. In Willy Schumann's hometown, there was one Jewish family. They owned the Haus T., a clothing store for men and boys.

Gentiles, including Willy and his family, shopped at the store regularly:

> My parents liked . . . the high quality of the merchandise and the reasonable prices . . . I remember the time my mother and I went to Haus T. to purchase a pair of short pants for me . . . As we approached the store we saw two

A parade of SA members, also known as storm troopers or brownshirts, march while holding Nazi flags as civilians on either side give the Hitler salute. Brownshirts were called such because of their brown uniforms.

young SA troopers in their yellowish-brown uniforms, high black riding boots, and peaked caps with chin straps in place. They had posted themselves to the left and right of the main entrance and were holding writing pads and pencils in their hands, quite obviously for the purpose of writing down the names of all customers entering the store. My mother hesitated briefly but then went in anyway, and we were not harassed by the SA men. The brightly lighted main business room was completely empty. Frau T. herself served us. When my mother asked a question about the lack of customers, she replied . . . "Nobody comes in anymore," and then she cried. On our way home, my mother was very quiet. After she had told my father about our experience, I remember that the mood in our house was of depression, and probably fear. It was the last time that any of my family went shopping in the Haus T.[5]

Other anti-Jewish actions in 1933 included the Law for the Reestablishment of the Professional Civil Service, which began removing Jews from government jobs. The Law Concerning Admission to the Legal Profession placed restrictions on Jewish lawyers and judges. Still, other laws put quotas on college admissions for Jewish students and restricted Jews from participating in the arts, owning land, and being newspaper editors.

This last prohibition changed the lives of Elizabeth Koenig and her family. Elizabeth's father was a very well-known journalist in Austria:

At that time [when Hitler became chancellor], my father had moved his family; my brother, myself, and my mother to Berlin, and when the Nazis came to power, we lived [in the city]. He [Koenig's father] was very . . .

24

endangered because he was . . . on the Nazi blacklist as a liberal writer and journalist.

I didn't know [about the blacklist] at the time. My parents didn't tell me . . . I only knew that we packed in a hurry and left Berlin as soon as possible which was easy for us because we had Austrian passports . . . My father had lost his job. And so . . . our life became very restricted from that time on.[6]

Eleven-year-old Edith Reimer also found her life greatly restricted by the Nazis. To her, Hitler's coming to power "was the end of a happy, carefree childhood; a process of fast maturing began."[7]

Forced to Grow Up Fast

Thousands of Jewish young people had to mature quickly. The rise of Nazism forced them to take on responsibilities and experience stress that no child should ever have to deal with. Lore Metzger was twelve years old when her "joyous, happy childhood changed . . . with unbelievable speed after Hitler's rise to power." She remembered that

...[signs] bearing such menacing messages as "Jews are forbidden to enter here," appeared at the entrances of the swimming pool, the theaters, the parks, the movies, the zoo and all the restaurants.

Jewish homes were soiled with swastikas, the Nazi insignia, and hateful anti-Jewish slogans. Organizations informed their Jewish members that their presence was no longer permitted . . . [Every] so often, Jewish men as well as children were beaten up in the streets and over and over again we heard of smashed-in windows on our beautiful synagogue, or of overturned tombstones in the Jewish cemetery.[8]

The banner at the center of this 1933 photo can be translated as "[The person] who buys from the Jew is a traitor." This was part of an anti-Semitic campaign to exclude and financially destabilize Jewish businesses and families.

Carola Stern Steinhardt was not yet a teenager when Hitler came to power. She did not understand why her gentile friends abandoned her:

I had lots of German friends . . . sometimes one of my friends would go with me to synagogue, and I went with her to church. My mother told me I shouldn't kneel down because that's not in my religion, so I didn't. Nobody bothered, I don't even think they did kneel down . . . But, I went to church Sundays and [my friend] went to synagogue on Saturdays. We were really close friends . . . But it changed in 1933. It changed a lot . . . This particular friend didn't change too much, but I had one girl which really was my idol. She was extremely intelligent, and she was a little redhead and she was very cute. And we played together, and at one point she said to me, "You know, Carola, I can't play with you anymore." And I said, "How come?" She said, "Because you're a Jew." I said, "What is that?" She said, "Well have you heard of Hitler?" I . . . said yes . . . because every morning they used to say Heil Hitler. "But why can't you play with me anymore? Why?" She said, "Because my father told me that you're Jewish, and . . . Aryan kids can no longer play with the Jewish kids" . . . Then suddenly . . . the whole group [of non-Jewish friends] disappeared. Nobody would play with a Jewish child anymore. So then we were all Jewish kids, and we stuck to one another.[9]

Disruptions Large and Small

Jews became fearful of going to synagogue or participating in Jewish religious rites and celebrations. In a later oral interview, survivor Walter F. recalled his bar mitzvah, a rite of passage in which a boy assumes the religious and spiritual responsibilities of an adult:

> I was supposed to be bar mitzvahed in 1933, in June shortly after [I became] thirteen, but that was right after the seizure of power by the Nazis, and things were very unsettled. Everybody was nervous, what are we going to do, [are] we going to bar mitzvah or not bar mitzvah, and a bar mitzvah normally was a big affair. Normally my bar mitzvah would have been an affair of 500 people, 1000 people I don't know what. Family from all over, from Mannheim, from Darmstadt, from Bebra, from Kassel, from Eisenach, so what are we going to do, we're not going to have a big bar mitzvah. Maybe we're not going to have a bar mitzvah at all. Finally they, my parents, decided we were going to have my bar mitzvah in January 1934, which was about seven or eight months later. And that bar mitzvah was very small. There were maybe 30 people. Twenty-nine Jews . . . one non-Jew. That man represented the Gestapo [secret police]. He was in the temple. They wanted to make sure the rabbi didn't say anything offensive.[10]

In some cases, the realization of change came from a small event rather than a major one. For Alfred Feldman, it came from "a small, inconspicuous event" in the city of Cologne:

> I had arranged to meet Aunt Betty in a public square. . . . When I arrived, she was not alone. A woman walked alongside the baby carriage, berating my aunt for having sat on a public bench. Aunt Betty angrily countered that she paid her taxes and had as much right to sit there as anyone else. The woman left in a huff, and we observed that, having reached the far side of the square, she talked

This copy of *Der Stürmer*, a Nazi newspaper, is from 1937. The primary headline reads "Judaism against Christianity," with a political cartoon showing an anti-Semitic caricature of a giant Jew smiling as Christ hangs on the cross.

to a policeman. Aunt Betty thought it prudent to leave the square.

As we passed a newsstand, she showed me . . . an issue of *Der Stürmer* [an anti-Semitic newspaper] . . . its bold headlines proclaiming some outrage committed by Jews, caricatured there with large noses, devious eyes, and hairy profiles evoking the face of sheep.

Within me, feelings of indignation welled up at the malice, the insult, the calumny [false charges] of the thing. It evoked a sense of being snubbed, of having been chastened [punished] that was not without fear.[11]

When President Paul von Hindenburg died on August 2, 1934, Hitler stood ready to do what he believed had to be done. Hitler, along with members of the Nazi Party within the German government, had already stripped the Reichstag, or the parliament of Germany, of its power to make laws. With von Hindenburg dead, Hitler made the next move: claiming the presidency for himself and combining it with the chancellorship. Thus, he became Führer and Reich chancellor, the supreme leader of the German nation.

Chapter 2

Jews Become Targets

Soon after the German parliament lost most of its law-making ability, all political parties other than the Nazi Party were outlawed, and Nazis took over the entire government. Once Hitler became the supreme leader of Germany, there were no government structures or officials left to stand in his way. He and other members of the Nazi Party were free to extend their racist, anti-Semitic political campaign throughout Germany with unprecedented pace and intensity.

In September 1935 at the Nazi Party's annual rally in Nuremberg, Adolf Hitler called on Nazi lawmakers in the German government to pass two major anti-Semetic laws, which together would become known as the Nuremberg Laws. One of these stripped Jews and anyone with Jewish blood of their German citizenship. The other outlawed marriage between Jews and "Aryans" in order to maintain the "purity" of the non-Jewish German populace. These laws had an enormous impact on German Jews; because they were no longer considered citizens, it was even easier for Nazi officials to take away their other basic rights.

Forced Identification

The Nuremberg Laws led to disputes over who was—and who was not—to be considered a Jew. On November 14, 1935, the Nazis added a new decree to clarify any questions of Jewish identity:

> Partly Jewish is anyone who is descended from one or two grandparents who are fully Jewish by race . . . A grandparent is to be considered as fully Jewish if he belonged to the Jewish religious community . . . A [full] Jew is he who is descended from at least three grandparents who are fully Jewish by race . . .
>
> Only the Reich citizen, as bearer of full political rights, exercises the right to vote in political affairs, and can hold a public office . . . A Jew cannot be a citizen of the Reich. He has no right to vote in political affairs, he cannot occupy a public office.[1]

In order to enforce anti-Semitic laws, Nazi authorities wanted to recognize Jews immediately and under all circumstances. Starting on October 5, 1938, Jewish passports had to be stamped with a red "J" for *Jude*. On September 1, 1941, Jews had to begin wearing big Jewish stars on their clothes. As Dora Kramen Dimitro, a Jewish survivor said: "We wore yellow stars so they should know who is a Jew, and we walked on the street too, not on the sidewalk . . . This was different because they had to know that we are Jewish."[2]

Henry Landman was fifteen years old when the Nuremberg Laws went into effect. Later, he recalled the impact on his family and friends:

> With one single stroke of the pen, my family lost its German citizenship. All Jews, even those listed as

Hitler salutes at the Nazi rally at Nuremberg on September 2, 1933. The rows of Nazi soldiers carry flags with the swastika, while high-ranking Nazi officials follow Hitler.

"quarter Jews," were deprived of their status as citizens and relegated to "subjects" of the State. We could not marry outside our own faith.

Slowly and deliberately, we lost all status within the German State. In time, we would not even be allowed to buy food from the same store as an Aryan . . . The Nuremberg Laws wiped out any . . . sense of equality that we may have [held]. We were stripped of our rights and, in time, our property. . . .

A Jewish man and woman wear the Star of David on their coats. This picture was taken in 1945, after Budapest was liberated by the Soviet army, meaning this couple survived the war.

In 1938, Heinrich Himmler, the powerful head of the SS [Nazi special security force] made the Jews sell their land and possessions to the Germans—at a lower price. We were forced to take our valuables to a . . . city clerk, who dutifully and efficiently gave you a receipt. No one on either side of that desk . . . expected to see those valuables ever again; but you had to go through the sham transaction. There was no choice. By involving the German citizens as recipients of the Jewish jewelry, lands, and factories, the Third Reich guaranteed the cooperation of the Germans themselves, since they would get the profits of the lower sale price.[3]

By 1938, no Jew could ride a train, go to restaurants with gentiles, nor attend classes. Even driver's licenses were revoked. By official decree, all Jews also had to have recognizably Jewish first names: "Insofar as Jews have given names other than those which they are permitted to bear . . . they are required as from January 1, 1939, to take an additional given name; males will take the given name Israel, females the given name Sara . . . "[4]

Terror and Violence Escalate

Easier identification led to greater persecution. One teenager recalled how the growing danger forced his family to seek an escape:

There was a young man whom we knew from the swimming pool and when it was still open to Jews we would go swimming there, my brother and I, and one time, a young fellow about our age started beating us up and if we had really resisted that would have made it worse . . . [There were many things] that we couldn't do anymore. There were many places where you couldn't go on vacation anymore. These were mild things, but being beaten up at the swimming pool, I felt it was getting worse and worse. My parents [thought so] as well, and so in 1936 . . . they made serious efforts to contact our relatives in St. Louis in order to try getting us out.[5]

In addition to suffering from random violence, more Jews were arrested by the Gestapo, a secret police division of the SS. Eve Nussbaum Soumerai recalled her terror one autumn day in 1937, when her father went out on an errand and did not return:

On . . . Sunday . . . Papa disappeared. He had left his brother Max, who was making arrangements to leave for Shanghai via Italy, and was on his way home . . . Mama sat by the window till it got dark. I could hear her muffled sobs during the night . . . Papa's "comrade" attorney Johann von Ledersteger, who also owned our apartment, promised Mama he would do all he could to locate Papa, whom he supposed had been in a roundup. "Berthold," he said, "received the Iron Cross . . . that should help."

I was devastated. My father, my best friend, was gone . . . After ten long weeks, Papa returned with his belongings in a cardboard box tied with string . . . [everyone] listened intently to what had happened to him in . . . prison. "The food was terrible: watery soup and stale bread. But we had cards, played Skat, and told funny stories." It sounded like a vacation in Switzerland. We had done all the suffering, or so it seemed. That night when Papa once again sat on my bed, I challenged him and came straight to the point. "We missed you. We were afraid. Mama cried all night. I suffered too." I was a little vague as to how I had suffered. Papa was silent.

"Didn't you miss us? Weren't you sad? How could you enjoy yourself like you said you did?"

After a long silence, Papa said, "Evchen, this might be difficult for you to understand, but it is possible to play cards, tell jokes, laugh, and be frightened all at the same time. You laugh and feel like crying. But when you laugh, you make others laugh. And suddenly there is hope. You feel the energy of laughter and friendship. And most important, you become the leader. You stand tall. And you know what, you will make a dent in setting things right. It's your form of resistance. Sorrow, outrage, infinite sadness, yes, tears, too, are ever present, but you are in charge, in charge of your laughter and your sorrow. Remember that always." And he tucked me in tighter than usual and left the door ajar so that I could see the light in the living room.[6]

Jews were not the only ones singled out by the Nazis. Roma and Sinti, often referred to as Gypsies, and people of African heritage were considered racially inferior to "Aryans" and therefore also treated with violence and cruelty. Others were marked because of their religious beliefs, sexual orientation, or political opinions.

Edith Gerder Reimer remembered the fate of one non-Jewish classmate:

Her father was a member of the Communist Party. Rather than live under the Nazis, he decided to kill his entire family. Evidently he had discussed this dramatic action with his wife. The day before the murder-suicide the girl came to class as usual, but during a short recess, she suddenly . . . announced quite gaily, that [she would] not be in school the next day, because her father was going to kill the whole family, [including] herself.

Ernst Thalmann leads a meeting of the Communist Party in Germany in 1931. The hammer and sickle symbol of the Communist Party can be seen in the star on the podium.

Nazi Ideology Beyond Germany

Identifying and isolating Jews played an important role when Germany annexed new territories. In 1938, Austria became part of the new German Reich. It happened quickly without a single shot being fired. When German troops marched into Vienna, the capital, on March 12, crowds of cheering Austrians greeted them.

Jewish young people soon found their world turned upside down: friends deserted them, schools expelled them, strangers accosted them in the streets. Anti-Jewish measures plunged their families into poverty. Before the annexation, about 192,000 Jews lived in Austria, and Vienna was an important center of Jewish culture and education. But by December 1939, only 57,000 Jews remained. Many had fled the country.

In October 1938, the Nazis took over the Sudetenland region of Czechoslovakia. Once more, Hitler took the territory without fighting for it, and again, more anti-Semitic measures followed. Magda Lipner remembered that her

> happy life changed suddenly after 1938 . . . The Germans marched in [triumphantly] . . .
>
> A few months later my father lost his permit to operate our shipping and moving co. He did continue work illegally and [got] many fines. We lost our financial security. We haven't had enough income. My father started to sell different items at home. Like cooking oil . . . My father didn't have enough money . . . he borrowed from his second cousin, and he gave as collateral a small diamond pendant. I found this out only after the war, when he returned it to me.[8]

... Not one of us took her seriously; I doubt that she, herself, was fully aware of the tragedy.[7]

Berlin's Night of Broken Glass

Nazi propaganda focused heavily on demonizing Jews, and much of the violence and cruelty Jews suffered was framed as righteous violence against evil, foreign invaders, even though the persecuted Jews were just as German as their tormentors. On the night of November 9, 1938, two days after Herschel Grynszpan had shot and killed a German diplomat in Paris, France, the Nazis saw a chance to use Grynszpan's actions against the Jewish community. They staged violent demonstrations and claimed that they were spontaneous acts of revenge by outraged German citizens. Rioters burned synagogues and destroyed Jewish-owned shops. They smashed so many windows that broken glass lay like snowdrifts on the sidewalks, giving the rampage its name: Kristallnacht, or "The Night of Broken Glass." Ernest Fontheim, a Jewish high school student, saw horrors that he would never forget:

> Thursday, November 10, 1938, started like any other day, I left our apartment on Kaiserdamm in the West end section of Berlin at around 7:20 for the nearest rapid transit . . . a half-mile walk past apartment buildings and one-family villas. There were no signs of any unusual activities. From there I took the train for a 15-minute ride to the Tiergarten Station in central Berlin near the high school of the orthodox congregation Adass Yisroel where I arrived a few minutes before the beginning of the school day at 8 o'clock. When I entered my classroom, some of my classmates were telling horror stories of what they had seen on their way to school like

smashed store windows of Jewish-owned shops, looting mobs, and even burning synagogues. A fair number of students [were] absent. The 8 o'clock bell rang signaling the beginning of classes, but no teachers were in sight either in our class or in any of the other classes along our corridor. That had never happened before. I don't remember anymore how long it took for the teachers to emerge from the teacher's conference room [but it] finally opened and the teachers streamed out to their various class rooms, they all looked extremely grim.

When our teacher Dr. Wollheim entered the room and closed the door, all talking stopped instantly, and there was complete silence in the class…In a tense voice Dr. Wollheim announced that school was being dismissed because our safety could not be guaranteed. This was followed by a number of instructions which he urged us to follow in every detail. Number one, we should go home directly and as fast as possible without lingering anywhere or visiting friends so that our parents would know that we are safe. Number two, we should not walk in large groups because that would attract attention and possible violence by hostile crowds. He concluded by saying that there would be no school for the foreseeable future and that we would be notified when school would reopen again.

I quickly walked back to the Tiergarten Station and decided to look out the window when the elevated train would pass the Synagogue Fasanenstrasse where I had become Bar Mitzvah . . . I literally felt my heart fall into my stomach when I saw a thick column of smoke rising out of the center cupola. There was no wind, and the column seemed to stand motionless reaching into the heavens. At that moment all rationality left me. I got off the train at the next stop and raced back the few blocks as if pulled by an irresistible force. I did not think of Dr. Wollheim's instruction nor of any possible danger to myself. Police barricades kept a crowd of onlookers on the opposite sidewalk. Firefighters were hosing down adjacent buildings. The air was filled with the acrid smell of smoke. I was wedged in the middle of a hostile crowd which was in an ugly mood shouting anti-Semitic slogans. I was completely hypnotized by the burning synagogue and was totally oblivious to any possible danger. I thought of the many times I had attended services there and listened to the sermons all of which had fortified my soul during the difficult years of persecution. Even almost six years of Nazi rule had not prepared me for such an experience.

Suddenly someone shouted that a Jewish family was living on the ground floor of the apartment building across the street from the synagogue. Watching the fire, the crowd was backed against the building. Someone else shouted: "Let's get them!" Everyone turned around. Those closest surged through the building entrance. I could hear heavy blows against the apartment door. In my imagination I pictured a frightened family hiding in a room as far as possible from the entrance door— hoping and praying that the door would withstand, and I prayed with them. I vividly remember the crashing violent noise of splintering wood followed by deadly silence, then suddenly wild cries of triumph. An elderly bald-headed man was brutally pushed through the crowd while fists rained down on him from all sides accompanied by anti-Semitic epithets. His face was bloodied. One single man in the crowd shouted: "How cowardly! So many against one!" He was immediately attacked by others. After the elderly Jew had been

During Kristallnacht, many Jewish homes, businesses, and places of worship were destroyed. This synagogue was set on fire during the Night of Broken Glass by violent mobs of Nazi-sympathizing Germans.

pushed to the curb, a police car appeared mysteriously; he was put in and driven off. I left this scene of horror completely drained . . . and went home . . . What has remained and will forever remain in my memory is the image of the thick column of smoke standing on top of the center cupola of that beautiful synagogue and the bloodied bald head of an unknown Jew.[9]

Chance and Survival

The events of Kristallnacht unfolded without rhyme or reason; some people were killed, some imprisoned and beaten. For no particular reason, some escaped the worst. Eve Nussbaum Soumerai and her family were among the lucky ones:

In the afternoon of November 10th, without explanation, our teacher dismissed the class early, asking us to go straight home . . . None of [us] asked why—we were happy to go home early.

When I got off the streetcar on Wallensteinstrasse and walked the half- block toward our apartment house, I got the first inkling that this was to be an extraordinary day: the inside of the shul [synagogue] on the ground floor of the apartment house was being destroyed. Men were axing the benches and other furnishings. I walked up a flight of stairs and saw a physician's apartment being destroyed—furniture and chandelier. I was frightened. I continued up one more flight and rang the bell to our apartment. My mother ushered me in quickly and motioned me to be quiet. The shades to all our windows were drawn. Soon my brother Norbert, who had celebrated his Bar Mitzvah 13 months earlier, came home from school. My parents then discussed a strategy for dealing with the Nazis, who, according to my parents, were sure to pay us a call . . . [and] would be looking for money and other valuables. My parents mainly [worried] about . . . two bank books [for accounts containing] the funds we needed [for] passage to the United States. We expected to [go] in December, when our quota numbers for the American visas were due to come up . . . My mother sewed the . . . bank books . . . into [our pajama tops] . . . My brother and I went to bed early, as my parents hoped that the Nazis would neither disturb the children nor discover the bank books. My mother prepared 30 marks in cash to turn over when they asked for money. My parents stayed up and waited.

[The Nazis] came at 11 o'clock . . . I was fully awake, but pretended to be asleep. They asked for money and my mother gave them the 30 marks. They then searched all the rooms, including the room my brother and I were in, and took all the jewelry and silverware they could find . . . They did not disturb us children and did not find the bank books.

Finally before they left, I heard them ask my father to put on his coat—he was to go with them . . . My father pleaded that he had never done anything wrong and that an Austrian colleague of his who had been a long-standing member of the Nazi party would vouch for him . . . At long last, the men left—miraculously without my father.

The next day we learned that my father was the only adult male resident of the apartment house who had been spared; all the other men, about 20, had been taken away—to Dachau . . . By the time we left . . . for the United States . . . the men had not returned.[10]

Friend Against Friend

Kristallnacht was a turning point for Eve Nussbaum Soumerai. It represented the end of a lifelong friendship:

> Best friends, true friends, are a necessity your whole life, whether you are young or old. Best friends listen to your secrets and worries and are always there to help you. You never need to tell them a lie because they are on your side and understand everything.
>
> Adelheid was my very best friend. Our mothers met when they were carrying us in their respective stomachs. Adelheid believed that we had met in another life because we were so close and knew each other so well that we did not even have to talk . . . Our mothers were also friends. They shared recipes, books, and secrets.[11]

Adelheid began to change after she joined the Bund Deutscher Mädchen (BDM):

> She loved going to meetings and told me on a few occasions how much fun they were. We were still talking but she started to inject bits of awful news, such as she had heard that Mama's favorite author Stefan Zweig's books were burned in a big fire, and that's when I knew for sure she had begun to hate me.[12]

Shortly after Kristallnacht, Adelheid came to Eve's house:

> I was alone when the doorbell rang. Adelheid, in full uniform, stood outside . . . Without a greeting of any kind, she demanded that I hand over all the photos taken of us together since we were babies. I was unable to move.
>
> "You know where they are, hurry up," she said. When I still did not move, she added, "They are in that

Hitler and the Nazi leadership censored the press and banned books that dissented with their views. Illegal books were then burned in fires, like this one at the University of Berlin.

cigar box in the bottom draw of your [dresser], in case you forgot." Was it my imagination or was she sneering? "Get them or I will." That did it. I ran to my room while she stayed at the door. A minute later I came back with the cigar box in which I kept my photos and spilled the contents on the floor. Photos of Adelheid and me as babies mixed in with those of my family greeted us, smiling. There was one of our first day of school, each of us carrying one of those large, decorated cones filled with goodies and licking chocolate lollipops . . . Adelheid knelt down, tore the photos into many pieces, spilled them on the floor, and yelled, "You people are like rats," and left running.

I picked up the bits of photos, put them back into the cigar box, and locked myself in my room and cried until I had no tears left. Her words had devastated me. We had been best friends ever since we were babies. What happened? We were rats? How can you change from best friend to a rat? These questions have preoccupied me for most of my life. On this day they came into sharp focus.[13]

From personal tragedies like a shattered friendship to assaults on whole Jewish communities, Kristallnacht was a turning point. Many Jews who had not planned to leave Germany decided that emigration was their only hope—if only a safe haven could be found. Unfortunately, the few safe havens that existed were open to only a relatively small number of Jews. As Germany moved toward war, Jews who could not escape found themselves trapped by the Nazis, who wanted to destroy them.

Chapter 3

The Nazification of Schools

Although Nazification, the process of imposing Nazi standards and ideals on German society, could be seen in all aspects of German life, it was particularly evident in schools. Hitler held a strong belief that converting young people to Nazi thinking was a key part of transforming Germany into a utopian Nazi state. He also thought that young men represented the future of society. "I begin with the young," he once said. "We older ones are used up. We are rotten to the marrow . . . But my magnificent youngsters! Are there any finer ones in the world? Look at these young men and boys! What material! With them, I can make a new world."[1]

Schools were a central place of Nazifications, both because young people spend so much time in school and because they're far more easily influenced by the state than when home. Nazified schools brought young people face-to-face with a new order that favored propaganda over education and imposed its racial policies on both students and faculty. Classes were transformed to reflect prejudiced

Nazi beliefs and policies, and many curricula were changed because certain books and ideas had been outlawed. Even outside classes, school was different. Physical education took on new meaning, and teachers and administrators were encouraged to make school as uncomfortable as possible for Jews and other "enemies of the state." Like life in general, life at school was divided into before and after Hitler.

"Heil Hitler"

In most schools, the first evidence of change was the so-called "Hitler salute." According to survivor Henry Landman:

> It became a law of the school that you had to salute every teacher with the new, but now well known, salute of the extended hand and open palm. "Heil Hitler" would be said with a stern and proud voice as you passed a senior faculty member. In time, more and more faculty would wear a uniform and the corridors were loud with the sounds of "Heil Hitler!" . . . This would tear through me; I would [shudder] every time that I heard it; I would feel sick when I had to say it. Hearing the salute would make me realize that I was truly an outsider . . . in the country of my birth![2]

For Simone Arnold Liebster, the salute became a special problem. She was a Jehovah's Witness; saluting the Nazi flag or saying "Heil Hitler" was against her religion. Despite persecution, she would not conform to the Nazi ideology of hate. This put her at odds with the Nazis:

> [Every morning], the whole class got up. During the singing of the national anthem, Deutschland über alles,

the *Horst-Wessel-Lied*, and other Nazi songs, everyone had to salute with arms outstretched. Mr. Ehrlich ran around with his ruler hitting any child whose arm started drooping. My arm never went up in spite of the physical reminder. The whole class was terrorized. [The teacher] ordered me: "You'll not leave my class until you write the words of each song ten times!" But the clock ran out. Escaping the morning ordeal, the children ran out as fast as they could. I stayed behind, but he sent me out. I went down slowly and very [fearfully]. Outside they waited for me. Mr. Ehrlich opened the window to watch with satisfaction as peer pressure came down on me. Mute and frightened, I faced the other children. They stared at me. Finally, a voice said, "Keep resisting that swine!" All repeated, "Resist, resist." Upstairs the window slammed shut. I still had no words.[3]

Acts of resistance rarely found this kind of support. This was especially true for Jewish students like Walter F.:

[After] Hitler [came to power] . . . they started school with the teacher coming in and everyone jumping up and [saying] "Heil Hitler!" . . . Of course you didn't want to be left out so everyone raised his hand, including myself . . . We had . . . one teacher who was teaching biology, chemistry, and physics . . . Dr. B. He was an old Nazi . . . [that meant] someone who joined the Nazi party back in the early 1920s. As a result he wore not just a swastika but a swastika in gold. This was a big deal for those guys . . . he was teaching [genetics], dominant and recessive genes and all that . . . he [taught that] all the recessive genes were in the Jews, and the Jews were bad . . . [He] was always giving me a bad grade. That's the only time I ever got a 3-, you know 1 was for best, 5 was for the worst grade, 3- was pretty bad from my

Students were required to perform the Nazi salute, regardless of their religion. In this picture, young girls make the salute at a military parade of the SA. SA members can be seen in the background in uniform.

point of view. I was always at least a 2+ sort of student. [Dr. B] was the only one I was . . . having . . . troubles with . . . [Still], I left high school because either that or they would tell me to get out. . . . they were trying to get rid of Jewish students.[4]

The New Nazi Curriculum

During the Nazi era, everything schools taught was subject to Nazi approval. In keeping with Hitler's ideas about hardened, tough-as-steel German youth, physical education took a central place in the curriculum. For boys, classes began to seem like basic training for the army.

Academic subjects got pushed aside, and the remaining lessons were changed to reflect what the Nazi

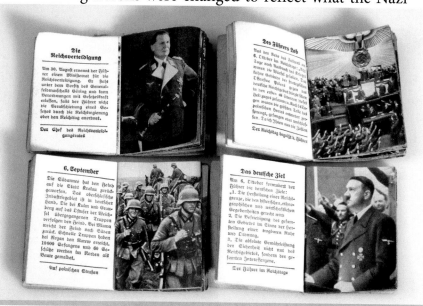

These booklets are magazines linked to Winterhilfswerk or "Winter Relief," a charity funded by the Nazis. Welfare work was an important part of the Nazi regime, and magazines publicizing that work also served as important propaganda for the party.

Textbook Anti-Semitism

Nazi education was explicitly aimed at indoctrinating German youth with the desired attitudes. Even picture books for young children taught hatred and mistrust of Jews. Books as seemingly innocuous as arithmetic textbooks also helped to indoctrinate a new generation of warriors. For example, one math problem used the following scenario:

A squadron of 346 bombers drops [fire] bombs on an enemy city. Each aeroplane carries 500 bombs [weighing] 1-1/2 kilograms each. Calculate the total weight of their bomb loads. How many fires will be caused if 30 per cent of the bombs are hits and only 20 per cent of hits cause fires? Day bombers fly up to 280 kilometers an hour, night bombers up to 240. Calculate the flying time from Breslau to Prague.[5]

Nazified education had two main goals: instilling in young people a hatred of Jews and other "subhuman" people and creating a new generation of soldiers, more military-minded than any generation before.

administration determined could and could not be taught. Many classes became less rigorous as a result. For example, in literature and composition classes, teachers could not use any of the twenty thousand books incinerated in the book burning of May 10, 1933. They could not allow students to express controversial opinions in their compositions. Both students and teacher had to adhere to Nazi ideology in and out of class.

In history, and especially in science, teachers had to present Nazi ideas as fact. This requirement created the most changes to biology, where racial science became the core of the curriculum. Throughout history, people have used science to excuse their prejudices, convincing themselves that other people are "less human" because of things like race, head shape, and facial features, even though none of these things indicate anything about someone's personality or intellect. Nazi biology was based on the idea that the "Aryan race," meaning the group of white Europeans of Germanic and Nordic descent, was superior to all others. For example, one particular chart was posted in almost every science classroom in Germany. This chart showed "Aryans" standing far above groups the Nazis called *Untermenchen*, or subhumans: Jews, Poles, Russians, and Africans.

For Hans Massaquoi, who grew up mixed race in Hamburg, racial science was not just something people learned in school; it directly threatened his existence:

> As a black person in white Nazi Germany, I was highly visible and thus could neither run nor hide, to paraphrase my childhood idol [boxer] Joe Louis . . . I was forced to develop my own instincts to tell me how best to survive physically and psychologically in a country consumed by racial arrogance and racial hatred and openly committed to the destruction of all "non-Aryans."[6]

Many Jewish students had to endure the humiliation of being used as object lessons in racial science classes. Generally, this involved choosing a student and pointing out which of their traits the Nazi Party considered inferior.

Bilder deutscher Rassen 1

Formen: Großwüchſig, ſchlank, langköpfig, ſchmalgeſichtig, Naſe ſchmal, Haar wellig

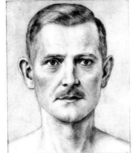

Nordiſche Raſſe

Farben: Sehr hell, Haar goldblond, Augen blau bis grau, Haut roſig-weiß

Formen: Sehr großwüchſig, wuchtig, langköpfig, breitgeſichtig, Naſe ziemlich ſchmal, Haar wellig oder lockig

Fäliſche Raſſe

Farben: Hell, Haar blond, Augen blau bis grau, Haut roſig-weiß

Formen: Kleinwüchſig, ſchlank, langköpfig, mittelbreitgeſichtig, Naſe ziemlich ſchmal, Haar wellig oder lockig

Weſtiſche Raſſe

Farben: Sehr dunkel, Haar ſchwarz, Augen ſchwarz, Haut hellbraun

The heading of the chart says "Pictures of German Races." It displays a Nazi racial hierarchy, with the "Nordic Race" at the top, the "Westphalian Race" in the center, and the "Western" or "Mediterranean Race" at the bottom.

Henry Landman recalled when this happened to one of his classmates:

> A teacher, who had been open in his hatred for the Jewish people, ordered one of my friends to the front of the class. Emanuel seemed surprised that he was being singled out in the middle of the biology class . . . I can see his face today as the teacher started to unravel the secret; my friend's crime was that he "looked Jewish." His features certainly were not those of the blond, blue eyed, demigod that the Third Reich favored; that alone was sufficient for this teacher to bring him in front of the class.
>
> "Do you see this boy, Class?" he asked as he pointed to my friend and turned him around like a display doll. The teacher spoke dispassionately, as if he were holding a glass jar with a specimen in it . . . "Do you see his big nose, his big ears, his thick glasses? Look at his lips. Look at him. This is what the Jew looks like! He is weak and dirty. I must warn you, for your own safety and health . . . if you see anyone like this, STAY AWAY from him. Do you hear?" His voice was not raised, but rather matter of fact. The Gentiles in the class stared at Emanuel the way one stared at a freak in the circus. They studied him from every angle as if they were trying to absorb the result for future reference. Some took notes. My friend had no choice but to stand there and wait until the teacher was through with him . . . Finally, the teacher dismissed him . . . Emanuel slowly walked back to his seat as all Gentile eyes followed him. None of the Jews could look at him.[7]

The teaching of racism did not stop in the classroom, or even in the Hitler Youth meetings. It made its way into music, movies, and books. For example, a picture book

This Nazi propaganda poster asks students to take up the cause and produce propaganda for the Nazi regime. The poster also calls for high schools to commit themselves to Nazi principles.

called *Trust No Fox in the Green Meadow and No Jew on His Oath* contained the following passage:

> When god the Lord made the World,
> He also created the races:
> Indians, Negroes, and Chinese
> Likewise the Jews, the evil beings.
> And [we] too, were also there,
> The Germans among the others.
> Then he gave to all a portion of the earth,
> That it might be cultivated by their labor.
> The Jew took no part in that work
> But from the very beginning, the devil seized him;
> He wished not to work, but only to deceive
> He was the ace of liars
> Learning quickly and well from
> his father the Devil . . .[8]

The Nazi ideas filtered into every aspect of youth's lives, from school to pop culture, and made anti-Semitism seem normal and unquestionable. People who started believing these ideas from a young age became key members of the Nazi Party.

Nazi Role Models

Part of Nazifying the schools meant replacing those teachers and administrators who were deemed unreliable with loyal Nazis. This had an immediate effect on student morale as well as education. Ezra BenGershôm wrote about the changes when a well-respected headmaster lost his job:

> For some reason, all the staff and pupils were assembled in the hall. Dr. Bergmann [the headmaster] mounted the rostrum [an elevated platform for public speaking] and began to address the school. Suddenly the sound of

heckling arose from among the massed ranks of pupils. Shocked people turned to see who had dared to interrupt the headmaster. The face they saw was a new one to the school. It belonged to the young officer in charge of the local Hitler Youth, who had taken a seat in the front row. He now rose to his feet and in front of the whole school ordered the headmaster to leave the rostrum . . . The unheard-of then occurred: Dr. Bergmann clearly felt obliged to comply with the order of the young man in uniform, whereupon the Hitler Youth leader took his place and announced that the headmaster had been dismissed for unreliability.[9]

In a different school, another "non-Aryan" boy drew unwelcome attention from a new principal. A new administrator at Hans Massaquoi's school, Herr Heinrich Wriede, made no secret of his contempt for Massaquoi's African heritage:

Herr Wriede came into my life—and I into his— sometime during my second school year . . . To introduce himself to us, he had the entire student body and faculty assemble in the schoolyard, where . . . he strutted around in high boots and riding breeches like a general inspecting his troops . . . [He said that] things would be done the Wriede way—if we knew what he meant. Of course we didn't know what he meant, but from the tone of his voice we got a pretty good idea that "the Wriede way" was nothing we'd be particularly crazy about.

As he paraded in front of us, he suddenly spotted me among the ranks of boys, and . . . fixed his hateful gaze on me.

"What I intend to instill in this school is pride in being German boys in a National Socialist German

Young girls help their teacher hang a photo of Hitler on the classroom wall, while Nazi flags hang on the chalkboard on October 19, 1938, in Germany. Symbols of Nazism were prevalent in schools throughout Germany.

state," he [said] without taking his eyes off me . . . After Wriede had finished and we returned to class, I couldn't rid myself of the unfamiliar and quite unsettling feeling of having just met a personal enemy, someone who wished me ill.[10]

Increasingly Hostile Conditions

Teachers who dared to defy the Nazi regime put themselves in danger of being fired, imprisoned, or both. Defiance could be anything from speaking out against the Nazis to being compassionate toward Jewish or other "non-Aryan" students.

Some teachers attempted to find a middle ground, stopping short of open defiance of Nazi rule with actions that could be explained away. For example, Walter F. talked about a teacher who developed an effective method of giving mixed messages:

[A] Nazi . . . named M [was] sitting next to me, and we were doing a test, a math test. Somewhere during the course of the test I was working away . . . and the teacher . . . said, "M, don't copy Jewish work" . . . M of course doesn't look at my paper [anymore,] he looks at his paper. After that . . . the teacher called me over and said, "You know I didn't want to offend you. I wanted to show up this Nazi . . . He's a big Nazi and he has to copy Jewish thinking. I didn't want to offend you."[11]

As teachers who could not accept the Nazi line quit or were fired, conditions grew worse for Jewish students. Lore Metzger recalled that Jewish students

were required to sit in a special corner of the classroom. During the recreation period we [had] to use a special place in the school yard in order not to get into physical contact with our fellow-students.

To have to sit in the so-called Jew corner, to have to listen to the most degrading remarks and to have to avoid all contacts with my classmates, who until now had been my friends, made these school years a period of torment and agony for me.[12]

On November 15, 1938, the government issued a formal order that banned Jewish students from all public schools. School had become such a horrible trial for Klaus Langer that he welcomed the news:

I did not realize at first that I no longer had to attend that awful school, with the "Heil Hitler" at the beginning and end of every lesson, [with] the way the teachers talked. Each day that I didn't have to attend school, I considered myself lucky.

I was not in the least bit sorry.[13]

After banning Jews from German schools, the Reich placed the responsibility for their education on the local Jewish communities. This became official in an addition to the Nuremberg Laws, dated July 4, 1939. It broke one of the last links between Jews and "Aryans" in Hitler's Germany.

Chapter 4

Gentiles Trapped within the System

As young Jews were increasingly persecuted in Nazi society, young gentiles, though not subject to the same cruelty as their Jewish peers, also found their ideas and actions restricted. Nazi leadership produced a steady stream of propaganda that told young people what to think, what to do, whom to admire, and whom to hate. Those who didn't conform were ostracized and subject to threats. Hitler wanted to shape young Germans into ideal soldier-like citizens. He made it clear how he thought German young people ought to be trained:

> My program for educating youth is hard. Weakness must be hammered away. In my castles of the Teutonic Order a youth will grow up before which the world will tremble. I want a brutal, domineering, fearless, cruel youth. Youth must be all that. It must bear pain. There must be nothing weak and gentle about it. The free, splendid beast of prey must once again flash from its eyes . . . That is how I will eradicate thousands of years

of human domestication. . . . That is how I will create the New Order.[1]

Hitler's "New Order" would be based on racism and anti-Semitism and would be created through warfare. He believed that society had become weak and that the only way Germany could regain dominance as a world power was by raising a generation of fierce, cruel young men. The New Order of Germans would act only for the good of the state and would not hesitate to hurt or even murder those who didn't fit into Hitler's vision of an ideal world.

Charisma and Omnipresence

Hitler used his considerable talent as an orator to glorify his plans and begin the Nazification of German life. His power over crowds soon became legendary.

Willy Schumann was eight years old when he first witnessed that power. It happened when Hitler's motorcade stopped briefly in Willy's hometown. People of all ages jostled one another, just hoping for a glimpse of the Nazi leader. In the commotion, Willy saw something he would never forget:

> For the first time in my life I experienced the phenomenon of a "mob" of people. It was a friendly, good-natured, and enthusiastic crowd, but a mob nevertheless. Individuals were no longer in control of their actions and movements . . . [Hitler] did not make a speech, there was no music, just hundreds of people who had come . . . to wave and cheer [him].[2]

Hitler did not rely upon public appearances to make himself known to the people. Schumann observed that

A member of the Hitler Youth, identifiable by his age and the swastika armband he wears, speaks to an adult soldier. The Hitler Youth called for extreme discipline and effectively served as a military training ground for the Nazi Party.

The Führer was ever-present for all Germans. He was [shown in] newspapers and . . . magazines, in some kind of pose at some activity. When we went to the movies, which at our age at the time had become a ritual, every Sunday afternoon in one of our two local theaters with the admission price of thirty Pfennig, there was always a short film [before] the main feature, sometimes a cartoon . . . [and also] the official newsreel of the week . . . [which always had] at least one segment showing the Führer "at work." But above all, Hitler's [constant presence] was made possible by the young broadcast medium of radio . . . Many millions of listeners could be . . . exposed to [an endless] series of mass rallies, parades, harvest festivals, opening ceremonies, memorial day celebrations, state funerals, and, above all, Hitler's speeches . . .

I have never in my life seen or heard a speaker with more magnetic talent . . . than Hitler; his effect on a mass audience was nothing short of hypnotic. But there was a side effect of my . . . exposure to a master speaker in my formative years. When the Third Reich collapsed and we young people slowly and very gradually began to reorient ourselves, create new values for ourselves, and look for new role models, I made a . . . discovery about myself. I was physically unable to . . . listen to a . . . speech in which the speaker shouts [at the audience] . . . This aversion to all noisy speech making has stayed with me to this day . . . I also know that many Germans of my age-group know and share this feeling.[3]

In telling his personal story, Willy Schumann treats official anti-Semitism almost as a nonfactor in his experience with his opinion:

Der Ewige Jude, which translates to "The Eternal Jew," was a book of propagandist photographs published in 1937 by the Nazis that depicted Jews as dirty and lazy. The cover shows an anti-Semitic caricature of a Jewish man.

How did we [young people] react to the never-ceasing anti-Semitic propaganda in the news media, in films, textbooks, and . . . contemporary works of literature? . . . these attempts at brainwashing were not effective. The image of "the Jew" remained strangely vague to us young people.[4]

All German young people had to deal with anti-Semitism in one way or another. The Nazis flooded Germany with anti-Jewish propaganda. In public, many young people simply parroted what they had heard described as "Jewish evil." In private, some of them struggled with their real feelings and took cues from parents and other family members.

Parental attitudes were important for Melita Maschmann. On her way to becoming an ardent Nazi, Maschmann noted her parents' almost casual anti-Semitism:

As children we had been told fairy stories which sought to make us believe in witches and wizards. By now we were too grown up to take this witchcraft seriously, but we still went on believing in the "wicked Jews." They had never appeared to us in bodily form, but it was our daily experience that adults believed in them. After all, we could not check to see if the earth was round rather than flat . . . The grownups "knew" it and one took over this knowledge without mistrust. They also "knew" that the Jews were wicked.

For as long as we could remember, the adults had lived in this contradictory way with complete unconcern. One was friendly with individual Jews whom one liked, just as one was friendly as a Protestant with individual Catholics. But while it occurred to nobody to be . . .

hostile to the Catholics, one was [hostile] to the Jews [as a group] . . . And when I heard that the Jews were being driven from their professions and homes and imprisoned in ghettos, the points switched automatically in my mind to steer me around the thought that such a fate could also overtake [my Jewish friends]. It was only the Jew who was being persecuted and "made harmless."[5]

Struggling with Government Propaganda

Jurgen Herbst also grappled with the anti-Semitism he learned at school and in the Hitler Youth. Years later, he remembered when his personal struggle began. The day after Kristallnacht, with the local synagogue still burning, Jurgen rushed home to tell his mother about it:

I described my walk to school in the morning, the broken window on the Lange Herzogstrasse with the half brick lying among the shoes, the burnt-out synagogue and the SS motorcycle . . . [the] fires for which no one would call the firefighters, and the story about . . . the Morgensterns on the Bahnhofstrasse. All during the telling my excitement rose. It had been such an incredible morning. I had heard such unbelievable tales. My cheeks were flushed. I felt my ears burn. How could all that have happened and what in the world did it all mean?

My mother, her back still turned toward me and her arms in the hot, soapy water, suddenly straightened up from her dishpan. She turned around slowly and looked me in the face, her arms now hanging straight down at her sides, water and soap bubbles dripping off them and forming puddles on the tiled kitchen floor. And then she said: "Do you know, Jurgen, if you had been Albert

75

Morgenstern, you would have been torn from your bed last night; you, your father, and I would have been pushed down the staircase, and all your toys and books would have been thrown on the street. Had you been born a little Jewish boy, this would have happened to you last night."

I was stunned. I did not know what to think. I could not get the picture out of my mind, the picture of my parents and me being pushed down the stairs. It stayed with me that day as I withdrew into my room to do my school assignments. I tried to read some chapters in my book on German sagas . . . but I could not concentrate. The picture came back, again and again.

It would recur, also, again and again, in the following months and years. It would return unexpectedly and unannounced. It would keep me awake at night, when I lay in my bed, and it would rise before me when, at [Hitler Youth] meetings or in Mr. Fuchtel's class, I would hear more about the "Jewish danger". . . It became very clear to me that what happened and what I had seen had something to do with Jews and Germans. But exactly what was it that made Jews so hateful to us Germans? I could not figure it out.[6]

When the war turned against Germany, Jurgen Herbst stopped believing in Hitler's vision of a thousand-year Reich. He kept most of his thoughts to himself, until one day he finally let his pent-up feelings spill out:

[It was] on a summer morning in 1944, not long before our school was closed . . . Fear gripped me with jolting intensity. The air-raid sirens had interrupted our lesson, we had descended into the basement, and after the all-clear had sounded we were waiting in our classroom for our teacher to reappear.

This is the last known photo taken of the Kusserow family, including Franz and Hilda (*center*) and their eleven children. They were Jehovah's Witnesses, and in 1936 the entire family was arrested and sent to various concentration camps.

As we sat idly on top of our benches, one of us started it: "Hermann Goring said that no British bomber will ever fly over our country."

Another added: "Der Führer said German soldiers do not know the word retreat."

And soon there was no stopping: "Our U-boats will totally isolate England." "Our Africa-Korps will soon join the Arabs in Jerusalem." "The [swastika flag] will forever wave over the Caucasus."

So it went, until the words escaped out of my mouth and I shouted: "This is how they lie!"

There was an abrupt, absolute stillness. My eyes fell on one of my classmates, who happened to be the son of our local SS chief. As I stared in his face, an ice-cold hand seemed to brush down my back. What did I say? What have I done? was all I could think.

The door opened and our teacher came in. "You are so quiet this morning," he said in mock astonishment. Then we turned to our lesson, and I slowly regained my composure. Nobody . . . ever mentioned the incident again.[7]

The Plight of Jehovah's Witnesses

Simone Arnold Liebster, the Jehovah's Witness who refused to give the "Heil Hitler" salute, did not fare so well. She faced a very painful choice: Give the salute or leave her school forever. The confrontation began with a summons to the principal's office:

I knocked timidly at the door . . . I heard "Come in" followed by "Heil Hitler." My throat tightened. I looked down at my feet, and I stood motionless in the doorway.

Under Suspicion

The Jehovah's Witnesses are members of a denomination of Christianity founded in the 1870s. Although Nazis valued Christianity, they were suspicious of Jehovah's Witnesses. Jehovah's Witnesses were opposed to war and had strong international connections. They also didn't value the state as highly as the Nazi regime expected its citizens to. The refused to allow their children to join the Hitler Youth, and they would not perform compulsory military-related tasks. Although on the whole Jehovah's Witnesses didn't take an explicit stance against Nazis, the Nazi regime was deeply suspicious of them, and Jehovah's Witnesses suffered severe persecution due to this suspicion.[8]

"Come over here. I'll read you a note from the city supervisor: "the student Simone Arnold refuses to salute. It is your duty to break her resistance or dismiss her from school." A long silence followed. Mr. Gasser stood up. He had an impressive stature:

"Why do you refuse?" I looked straight into his eyes.

"Because I'm a Christian."

His forehead wrinkled up with surprise, and he said, "So am I."

He picked up the city supervisor's letter again and threw it back down on the desk. He continued, "But you can't stay in our school unless you salute. If you refuse, it will be the end of a brilliant career. You'll become an outcast . . . and your learning capacity will be useless. Try to understand that, and don't make a foolish decision. You may go." It was a short and straightforward talk.[9]

Simone made her choice. When the other students gave the Hitler salute, she stood still, arms at her side. Shortly afterward, the school expelled her. Other Jehovah's Witnesses would suffer a much worse fate. Many were eventually sent to the concentration camps, and still others were simply killed for their beliefs.

On March 28, 1942, another Jehovah's Witness, twenty-year-old Wolfgang Kusserow, was executed for refusing to serve in the army. On the day before his execution, he wrote a final letter to his family:

My dear Parents, and my dear brothers and sisters!

One more time I am given the opportunity to write you. Well, now I your third son and brother, shall leave you tomorrow early in the morning. Be not sad, the time will come when we shall all be together again. "Those sowing seed with tears will reap even with a joyful cry" . . . So we confidently look forward to the future.

Dear Papa, I am sorry that I was not allowed to visit you early in December. Exactly one year ago from tomorrow I saw you and Hildegard for the last time. In the meantime I have visited Lenchen. It was a special joy for me to see Mummy once again.

Well, dear Mummy, Annemarie read me your dear letter during her visit . . . It is fine that you are busy in the baking factory (prison), so you are at least in a warm room and you have something to eat. Lenchen is now in the concentration camp.

Dear Annemarie, once more special thanks to you for all your endeavors. May our Lord reward you. I have you all constantly in mind . . . Satan knows that his time

A Romani couple at Belzec concentration camp. Romani are a traditionally nomadic ethnic group who live throughout the world but can be found primarily in Europe. The Romani people were also heavily persecuted by Nazis.

is short. Therefore, he tries with all his power to lead [people of good will] astray from God, but he will have no success. We know that our faith will be victorious.

In this faith and this conviction I leave you.

A last greeting from this old world in the hope of seeing you again soon in a New World.

"Your son and brother (signed) Wolfgang."[10]

The Jehovah's Witnesses were one of the other, smaller groups, like communists and Roma, who suffered deeply under the Nazi regime alongside Jews.

Difficult Choices

Defying Hitler and the Nazi government had deadly consequences. However, through propaganda and a Nazified Germany, the Nazis had managed to convince many Germans to help out in the war effort. Irmgard Paul was not yet a teenager when she faced a choice between her loyalty to Hitler and love for her anti-Nazi grandfather. She lived in Berchtesgaden, near Hitler's summer home. She had no contact with Jews or "other enemies of the Reich." Her moment of confrontation began with a school project for the war effort:

Monday mornings each pupil had to weigh in with at least two pounds of used paper and a ball of smoothed-out . . . aluminum foil to help with the war effort. Ingrid [my sister] and I were in fierce competition for the few scraps of foil and paper we could get our hands on in both grandparents' households and had difficulty meeting our quotas. [Mother] reused every available paper bag until it was torn to bits; the scanty newspapers were cut for toilet paper, and grocers would put everything unwrapped into our string bags.

One rainy day I had a brainstorm. We were playing in my grandfather's large, [dusty] attic, looking through the trade magazines that he had saved over the years. Suddenly I realized that here, right in front of us, were pounds and pounds of paper gathering dust . . . I had no doubt that [grandfather] would say yes . . . [I] hurried as fast as I could down the three flights of stairs into [his] workshop . . . [I asked] his permission to take his old journals to school for the recycling collection. He looked at me as if he had not quite understood my question and then said in a calm, icy tone that not a sliver of any of his magazines would go to support the war of that scoundrel Hitler. Disappointment and something akin to hatred must have shown on my face. How dare he not support the war that we were told everyday was a life-and-death struggle for the German people?

[Then one day] I accepted [my teacher's] invitation to have a special treat of hot chocolate and cookies at her house . . . I wondered why she had invited me. After a few [polite words] she asked point-blank what my grandfather thought about Adolf Hitler and what he said about the war. I was still angry with my grandfather but stalled . . . weighing my feelings against my answer. On the one hand, [Grandfather] was withholding paper for the war effort . . . On the other hand, he was my grandfather.

After much too long a pause I [decided] that I liked this nosy teacher less than my grandfather . . . [I said] that I did not know what he thought and that he never said much anyway . . . and I assured her that he said nothing about the Führer . . . Although I did not know it that day, [the teacher] was a Nazi informer, and my telling the truth would have sent [my grandfather] to a concentration camp.[11]

Some young people made a different choice. Alfons Heck was thoroughly devoted to the Führer. He entered the Hitler Youth at the age of ten and worked his way through the ranks, becoming a senior leader by the time he was sixteen. He confronted his own demons after the July 20, 1944, attempt to assassinate Adolf Hitler:

> I had no mercy with the plotters. They were heinous criminals trying to stab [Germany] in the back . . . I learned only after the war that my own father had been detained overnight by the *Gestapo* [secret police] early in September and questioned about his connections to prominent former Social Democrats . . . He [did not] tell the *Gestapo* that he had fathered me, a leader of the Hitler Youth. If the *Gestapo* had found him involved in the slightest anti-Nazi activity, my status as a loyal adherent to the regime wouldn't have saved him. Despite our opposing views of Nazism, I did not want to see my father come to harm; but if he had plotted against Hitler I would have stopped him. Would I have sent my own father to a concentration camp and likely death? It's conceivable, although I like to think I would have given him one warning before calling the *Gestapo*.[12]

Sterilization and Euthanasia

Another part of the Nazi plan for a "master race" was killing people with hereditary disabilities, such as mental illness, physical deformity, epilepsy, blindness, and deafness. This began with a forced sterilization law enacted on July 14, 1933. However, the sterilization law was a forerunner for the so-called euthanasia killings that began in October 1939. Hitler issued a firm decree empowering physicians to grant "mercy deaths" to "patients considered incurable."[13]

Fearful of public reaction, the Nazi regime carried out these killings of patients in mental asylums and other institutions in secret. However, Germans heard many rumors.

Irmgard Paul remembered overhearing a conversation about a neighbor girl who disappeared:

> One afternoon . . . Tante [Aunt] Susi and my mother talked quietly with serious, worried faces. I loved to listen to grown-up gossip and moved closer to hear what the two women were saying. "One of the Dehmel children, the [mentally retarded] one that's never outside, was picked up by the Health Service a few weeks ago, and now they've said she's dead from a cold," said my mother. Tante Susi with her pretty bobbed haircut shook her head . . . "Well, it's probably true, her dying from a cold, I mean" . . . I began to pick some white, pink-rimmed daisies as I mulled things over. Just that morning I had played with [the other Dehmel children] and I knew they were fine. I began to wonder about the sister who had never played outside. What did it mean, she was taken away? She died from a cold? Would they take me away if I had a cold, and would I die too? I was infected by the feeling of unease I had sensed during the two women's conversation but, as quickly as they had, convinced myself that there was nothing to fear. Certainly Mutti and Vati [Mama and Papa] would never let anyone take me away.
>
> What I did not know, and what the adults refused to believe or face, was that Hitler's [killing] program, while still . . . hidden from the general public, was up and running. And if Mutti had . . . suspected foul play concerning the Dehmel baby, she would have convinced herself that Hitler himself would not condone such murder.[14]

After World War II, members of the Nazi regime were tried for a range of crimes against humanity by an international court. At the Dachau Trials in 1945, Eugen Seybolu (*right, pointing*) identifies Fritz Hintermeyer (*left, standing*) as the doctor who presided over the execution of Soviet prisoners of war.

The drive to Nazify the German nation and purify the "Aryan" race turned German society upside down. It forced Germans of all ages, races, and religions to deal with Nazism in one way or another. Those who lacked enthusiasm for the Führer and his empire often ended up in concentration camps. Political enemies of the Nazis—communists and socialists—were put in camps. After Kristallnacht, the Nazis deported Jews to concentration camps in Germany.

Irmgard Paul remembered when the brother of her honorary aunt came to visit:

> We knew that [Ferdi] had just been released from Buchenwald, a new kind of prison called K.Z. . . . concentration camp. Tante Susi was visibly shaken on seeing how old and diminished he looked . . . I realized that the concentration camp was the worst thing that could happen to a person and decided I would never get into the kind of trouble that would send me there.[15]

Regardless of who they were or how they coped, the young people of Germany had to make difficult choices.

Chapter 5

Nazi Youth Organizations

Political youth movements were prevalent in the years following World War I, and the Nazi Party was no exception. The youth organizations linked to the Nazi Party largely went underground in 1923 after a failed attempt by Hitler to seize power in Munich, but once Hitler became the primary leader of Germany in 1933, youth groups resurfaced with strength and purpose.

The Hitler Youth developed alongside the Nazi Party, but it grew dramatically in importance after Hitler appointed Baldur von Schirach as youth leader of the German Reich in June 1933. Youth groups were crucial to keeping Nazis in power; they were viewed as the future of the Nazi Party and therefore of Nazi Germany. Members of the Hitler Youth were also viewed as future soldiers on behalf of the Nazi regime.

While the Hitler Youth was initially exclusively for teenage boys, other organizations developed to encompass all ages. There was the League of German Girls for girls, and eventually both the Hitler Youth and the League of German Girls were divided into subunits based on age.

Members of the Hitler Youth of all ages perform the Nazi salute at a Nazi rally in 1936. The Hitler Youth was open to boys ages ten to eighteen, and eventually it became compulsory for all eligible boys and young men.

To further the development of Hitler Youth groups, the Nazi Party outlawed all other organizations for young people, including any church-sponsored programs and sports leagues. Non-Nazi youth organizations disbanded or went underground.

Child Soldiers

In the beginning, membership was optional. The Hitler Youth Law of December 1936 forced all "Aryan" young people between the ages of fourteen and eighteen to join. Less than three years later, children had to join at the age of ten. Alfons Heck joined before membership became compulsory. Writing as an adult, he remembered looking forward to it:

> Far from being forced to enter the ranks of the *Jungvolk* [junior branch of the Hitler Youth], I could barely contain my impatience and was, in fact, accepted before I was quite 10. It seemed like an exciting life, free from parental supervision, filled with "duties" that seemed sheer pleasure. Precision marching was something one could endure for hiking, camping, war games in the field, and a constant emphasis on sports . . . There were the paraphernalia and the symbols, the pomp and the mysticism, very close in feeling to religious rituals. One of the first significant demands was the so-called *Mutprobe*: "test of courage," which was usually administered after a six-month period of probation. The members of my *Schar*, a platoon-like unit of about 40–50 boys, were required to dive off the three-meter board—about 10 feet high—head first into the town's swimming pool. There were some stinging belly flops, but the pain was worth it when our *Fahnleinfuhrer*, the

Pledging Allegiance

Young members of the Hitler Youth were asked to pledge their thoughts, lives, and even prayers to the Nazi cause and to Hitler. They took an oath, learned a pledge of allegiance, and recited Nazi prayers:

> The oath: In the presence of this blood banner which represents our Führer, I swear to devote all my energies and my strength to the saviour of our country, Adolf Hitler. I am willing and ready to give up my life for him, so help me God.
>
> The pledge of allegiance: I promise to do my duty in love and loyalty to the Führer and our flag.
>
> A prayer: Adolf Hitler, you are our great Führer. Thy name makes the enemy tremble. Thy Third Reich comes, thy will alone is law upon the earth. Let us hear daily thy voice and order us by thy leadership, for we will obey to the end and even with our lives. We Praise thee! Heil Hitler![1]

Adolf Hitler was treated almost like a god, and children were taught that he was a perfect, beloved leader. The idea was to convince even the youngest children that they could and should do anything Hitler and other Nazi leaders asked, to defend Nazi ideas at any cost. They were meant to be soldiers of the Nazi regime.

Youth organizations allowed the Nazi Party to indoctrinate children from a very young age. These small boys proudly stand in front of the Nazi flag.

15-year-old leader of our *Fahnlein* (literally "little flag"), a company-like unit of about 160 boys, handed us the coveted dagger with its inscription Blood and Honor. From that moment on we were fully accepted.[2]

Long after the war, Alfons Heck looked back on those days and realized what it had cost him:

The Hitler Youth demanded a lot of its members both physically and emotionally, and it was designed in many ways to be a paramilitary organization. At a summer camp on the Baltic coast, a group of Hitler Youth leave camp for a hike.

In Hitler's Germany, my Germany, childhood ended at the age of 10, with admission to the *Jungvolk*. Thereafter we children became the political soldiers of the Third Reich . . . Unless [children] have singularly aware parents, the very young become defenseless receptacles for whatever is crammed into them. We, who had never heard the bracing tones of dissent, never doubted for a moment that we were fortunate to live in a country of such glowing hopes . . . And unless one was Jewish, a gypsy, a homosexual or a political opponent of Nazism, the Germany of the '30s had indeed become a land of promise.[3]

The Constant Demands of Membership

Dogma and ritual worked together with near-constant activity to ensure that the Hitler Youth would play a dominant role in the life of every member. In 1938, an anonymous writer kept track of a typical day in a Hitler Youth camp:

> 4:45 Am get up. 4:50 gymnastics. 5:15 wash, make beds. 5:30 coffee break. 5:50 parade. 6:00 march to building site. Work until 14:30 with 30 minute break for breakfast. 15:30–18:00 drill. 18:10–18:45 instruction. 18:45–19:15 cleaning and mending. 19:15 parade. 19:30 announcements. 19:45 supper. 20:00–21:30 singsong or other leisure activities. 22:00 lights out.[4]

Even at home, the Hitler Youth demanded a great deal of its members, often taking time away from schoolwork and family obligations. Pressed by these demands, Jurgen Herbst could not keep up:

> [My] report cards in school began to reveal that I had entered on a slowly but steadily descending path. By

Easter 1940 my overall grade was still "good"; a year later it had dropped to "almost good." Thereafter my teachers continued to [say] that I had begun to slack off. Nevertheless, though I had also shown tendencies to become "disruptive," I still achieved "satisfying results." . . .

The . . . [main] cause of my academic decline was my growing involvement in the [Hitler Youth]. As I passed my fourteenth birthday, I advanced in the ranks step by step from being responsible for a *Jugenschaft* of ten to heading a *Jungvolk* of thirty and finally, as I turned sixteen . . . to command a *Fähnlein* of a hundred.[5]

The League of German Girls

Girls also marched and drilled. They played sports and received regular indoctrination in Nazi principles. Some girls tried to avoid joining; others, like Irmgard Paul, looked forward to it:

I was now completely focused on joining the Hitler Youth . . . I would be ten in May—far too old for *Kindergruppe*, I felt—and began to badger Mutti to ask Frau Deil if I could join the Jungmädel, the junior division of the female [Hitler Youth], that would lead me at age fourteen, to enrollment in the BDM (Bund Deutscher Mädchen), the next level of a girl's training and indoctrination. Yes, I knew I was the youngest in my grade, and yes, we were late with the application, but how could I tolerate it if all my friends were strutting around in their uniforms every Friday afternoon and I was left out? . . . Indeed, Frau Deil arranged for my entry.

At our first *Appell* (drill and meeting) we were lined up by size four rows deep and called to order for learning how to march in place . . . Finally, we . . . marched through town from one end to the other . . .

I was completely seduced by a feeling of belonging, of being united with all young Germans wearing this uniform . . .

In addition to marching drills we Jungmädel trained for sports competition, hiked, sang a great deal, and listened to many lectures and speeches by senior leaders. They always said that every boy and girl had to do his or her share to win the war and that we must believe that the Führer was invincible and Germany's only salvation. No one asked a question; it was not called for and we were much too well indoctrinated to do so.[6]

Feeling Excluded

Not all young people got caught up in the Hitler Youth. Some rebelled against its regimentation, and some fought its racism. Jews and other "non-Aryan" children did not face these choices; they were not allowed to join in the first place. Carola Stern Steinhardt and other Jewish girls did not understand why they were excluded:

We were little kids [and when we saw] . . . a circle of German girls who had these nice outings, we felt so why can't we be part of it. Why can't we be part of it? Why can't we? As a matter of fact, I remember at one point when . . . everybody said, "Heil Hitler" . . . I did, too. What did I know? I was eight years old. So my mother said to me, "You're not supposed to do that." I said, "Why not?" She said, "Haven't you been told that you are Jewish?" I said, "Oh, I forgot." So it was very hard to comprehend. I couldn't get it together that I was suddenly Jewish and I couldn't do whatever I did before.[7]

Members of Bund Deutscher Mädchen (the League of German Girls) pose in their uniforms. Like the Hitler Youth, the League of German Girls was open to children ages ten to eighteen.

For Hans Massaquoi, being excluded was even more of a shock. As part of a contest to see which class could enroll 100 percent of its students, the teacher drew a chart of the classroom, with a box for each student:

> Each morning, Herr Schürmann would [ask] who had joined the Hitler Youth . . . then gleefully add the new enlistees' names to his chart.
>
> One morning, when the empty squares had dwindled to just a few, Herr Schürmann started querying the holdouts as to their reasons for their "lack of love for Führer and *Vaterland* [Fatherland]." Some explained that they had nothing against Führer and *Vaterland* but weren't particularly interested in the kinds of things the *Jungvolk* were doing, such as camping, marching, blowing bugles and fanfares, and beating on medieval-style drums . . . When it came to what I thought was my turn to explain, I opened my mouth, but Herr Schürmann cut me off. "That's all right; you are exempted from the contest since you are ineligible to join the *Jungvolk*."
>
> The teacher's words struck me like a bolt of lightning. Not eligible to join? What was he talking about? I had been prepared to tell him that I hadn't quite made up my mind whether I wanted to join or not. Now he was telling me that, even if I wanted to I couldn't.[8]

After class, the teacher explained that only pure-blooded "Aryans" could join the Hitler Youth. Hans did not qualify because his father was African.

Organized Resistance

Many "Aryan" young people rejected the regimentation of the Hitler Youth: the uniforms, the endless marching, the pressure to conform to Nazi ideals. In the 1930s, some of these rebels created loosely organized groups, such as the Edelweiss Pirates and Swing Youth, or more informally, the Swing Kids. In general, the Pirates came from working-class backgrounds while most Swing Kids belonged to the upper-middle class.

Instead of marching in lockstep with the Hitler Youth, these sons and daughters of wealth and privilege liked to dress up in party clothes and dance the night away to American jazz and big band music. They were not political; they simply rejected the drab conformity of Nazi youth culture.

They also enjoyed shocking that culture. One unnamed Hitler Youth left a record of his reaction:

> The sight of some three hundred dancing people thrashing about was absolutely horrid. No one can describe the dancing because no one danced normally. Indeed, this was the naughtiest . . . dancing that can be imagined . . . Everyone jumped about like crazy while they mumbled English musical gibberish. The Band increased the tempo faster by the minute. No member of the band was sitting, because they were all getting hotter and wilder as they also succumbed to the jungle beat on the stage.[9]

By 1941, their loud partying and frenetic jitterbugging had drawn Nazi official attention. On August 18, police arrested more than three hundred Swing Kids. Those identified as leaders found themselves in the concentration camps for "un-German" activities or activities the Nazis did not tolerate. Instead of taming the Swing Kids, this official clampdown made them bolder. They still wanted

The Edelweiss Pirates emerged out of a counterculture movement that rebelled against the strict ideals of the Hitler Youth. Though primarily pranksters, they were also known to assist the Allied war effort and engage in anti-Nazi activities.

to have a good time, but they began handing out anti-Nazi literature and viewing their rebellion in another light.

The Edelweiss Pirates were rebels from the beginning. Many of them dropped out of school so they could avoid involvement with both the Nazi Party and the Hitler Youth. They engaged in activities that ranged from mockery of Nazi dogma to malicious mischief and even outright sabotage.

Walter Meyer became part of a Pirate group in the city of Dusseldorf:

> We had [meetings] generally at a cafe on . . . Kings Avenue in Dusseldorf [which is] one of the best known avenues in the world. It's gorgeous, wide, and has a

river in the middle and all chestnut trees and so on. Well there was a cafe and in the back of the cafe was a pool room . . . we used to play pool, and we had our little meetings there and . . . maybe one would say, "You know, the Hitler Youths . . . store their . . . equipment at such-and-such a place. Let's make it disappear." "Okay, when are we going to meet?" Such-and-such a time. And that's what we did. It . . . came to the point where people began to look for us because we went a little too [far] . . . you know we started maybe by deflating the tires, then we made the whole bicycle disappear, so it came to the point where [there were] too many complaints.[10]

The Pirates liked to make up their own words to Hitler Youth marching songs, a practice that infuriated the powers-that-be:

We all sat in the tavern
With a pipe and a glass of wine,
A goodly drop of malt and hop,
And the devil calls the tune.
*Hark the hearty fellows sing!
Strum that banjo, pluck that string!
And the lasses all join in.
We're going to get rid of Hitler,
And he can't do a thing. . . .
*Hitler's power may lay us low,
And keep us locked in chains,
But we will smash the chains one day,
We'll be free again.
We've got fists and we can fight,
We've got knives and we'll get them out.
We want freedom, don't we, boys? . . . .
Out on the high road, down in the ditch
There're some Hitler Youth patrolmen,

and they're getting black as pitch.
Sorry if it hurts, mates, sorry we can't stay,
We're Edelweiss Pirates, and we're on our way.
*We march by banks of Ruhr and Rhine [rivers]
And smash the Hitler Youth in twain,
Our song is freedom, love and life,
We're Pirates of the Edelweiss.[11]

The Pirates paid a high price for their activism. After a major roundup in the city of Cologne, the Nazis had thirteen Edelweiss Pirates hanged.

Crusading for the Truth

In the summer of 1942, a small group of students at the University of Munich formed a resistance group called the White Rose. Students Hans and Sophie Scholl, Christoph Probst, Alexander Schmorell, and Willi Graf and Professor Kurt Huber made up the small group. The White Rose published and distributed a series of anti-Nazi pamphlets. The fifth pamphlet, published in February 1943, dared to admit the truth; Germany was losing the war:

> A Call to All Germans!
>
> The war is approaching its destined end . . . in the East the [German] armies are constantly in retreat and invasion is [near] in the West. Mobilization in the United States . . . exceeds anything that the world has ever seen. It has become a mathematical certainty that Hitler is leading the German people into the abyss. Hitler cannot win the war; he can only prolong it. The guilt of Hitler and his [followers] goes beyond all measure. Retribution comes closer and closer.
>
> But what are the German people doing? They will not see and will not listen. Blindly they follow their seducers into ruin. Victory at any price! is inscribed on

their banner. "I will fight to the last man," says Hitler—but in the meantime the war has already been lost.

Germans! Do you and your children want to suffer the same fate that befell the Jews? . . . Are we to be forever a nation which is hated and rejected by all mankind? No. [Turn away] from National Socialist [Nazi] gangsters. Prove by your deeds that you think otherwise. . . . Cast off the cloak of indifference you have wrapped around you. Make the decision before it is too late . . . Do not believe that Germany's welfare is linked to the victory of National Socialism for good or ill. A criminal regime cannot achieve a German victory.

Hans Scholl (*left*) and his sister Sophie (*right*) were both members of the White Rose resistance group, which distributed anti-war pamphlets and resisted Nazi propaganda. In 1943, three years after these pictures were taken, they were arrested for high treason and executed.

Separate yourselves in time from everything connected with National Socialism. In the aftermath a terrible but just judgment will be meted out to those who stayed in hiding, who were cowardly and hesitant . . .

Freedom of speech, freedom of religion, the protection of individual citizens from the . . . will of criminal regimes . . . will be the [basis] of the New Europe.[12]

While distributing a sixth leaflet, the Scholls were arrested. On February 22, 1943, Hans and Sophie Scholl and Christoph Probst were beheaded. Graf, Schmorell, and Professor Huber were later arrested and executed.

Putting Young Lives on the Line

After Germany's defeat at Stalingrad on February 2, 1943, Nazi fortunes plummeted. By the summer of 1943, ten thousand boys younger than age seventeen began training to be soldiers.[13] Older members of the Hitler Youth found themselves called up to the front lines. These inexperienced boy soldiers did not fare well. Gerhardt Thamm remembered his mandatory service: "As a fifteen-year-old boy I fought briefly in a war. My fight was neither noble nor heroic. I saw the horrors that no fifteen-year-old boy should ever see. I came into war purely by unfortunate happenstance, and survived it purely by lucky coincidence."[14]

Training was brief and harsh. Gerhardt remembered being pushed to exhaustion during a simple run. After being told again and again to run faster, some of the boys could not keep up:

The formation started to stretch out. Some of the boys at the front faded and the formation began to disintegrate.

Finally some of the boys, white clouds of breath expelling from [their] lungs . . . slowed down and started to walk. In a flash . . . the sergeant rushed up and screamed . . . "Is this what the Hitler Youth has produced? A bunch of weaklings? Move it! Move it! . . . The Führer does not want weaklings! He wants Father land defenders! You are his last hope. Run!" . . . [Then] he watched as we, heaving, coughing, [struggled] to make the last circuit around the parade ground.

As we came out of the last turn [an] elderly soldier . . . surveyed the decrepit group and told us to get into formation . . . He reminded us that we were not a bunch of sheep, but German soldiers, and never to forget it. [Then] he turned and walked toward the sergeant, saluted, and [left]. The sergeant . . . walked totally around the platoon, returned to front and center, and spoke in an almost normal human voice. "I will make soldiers out of you! . . . You may think you are just a bunch of boys, but when I am through with you, you will be the most efficient killing machine the world has ever known—or you will be dead!"[15]

No one knows exactly how many boys died in combat, but there are statistics about particular units in certain battles. For example, of the ten thousand boys in Gerhardt Thamm's unit, only six hundred survived.[16] In April 1945, a unit of five thousand boys tried to defend the Pichelsdorf bridges into Berlin. Over a period of five days, all but five hundred boys were killed or wounded.[17] Like other survivors, these boy soldiers were left to face what their nation had become in pursuit of an evil dream.

Chapter 6

The "Final Solution" and the End of the War

Although many Jews had been murdered as Nazis attempted to create a Europe free of Jews, the Nazi plan didn't necessarily mean killing every Jew. All of that changed in January 1942. Jews had already suffered through being forced into the ghettos and concentration camps of Poland and subject to killing squads that slaughtered entire communities of Soviet Jews. In 1942, a group of high-ranking Nazis gathered in the resort town of Wannsee, Germany, and officially ordered the implementation of a plan to murder all the Jews in Europe. They called this the "final solution" to the Jewish problem.

In pursuit of this "final solution," death camps were created and Nazi efforts turned toward killing all Jews on a mass scale. Gas chambers that looked like shower rooms but dispensed poison gas rather than water operated day and night in the death camps; crematoria, or brick ovens for burning bodies, spewed dark smoke into the air. The smell of death spread everywhere.

Hitler sits in the foreground on the far left at a Nazi Party gathering in 1941. Next to him is Joseph Goebbels, the minister of propaganda for the Nazi regime.

A year later the war turned against Germany as Soviet troops crushed the German Sixth Army at Stalingrad. Many Nazi leaders took this as the beginning of the end for Hitler's Thousand Year Reich. They dared not voice this opinion, though; to do so would be treason. While the war effort faltered, the genocide of the European Jews picked up pace.

Increased Killing

When it became obvious to many Germans that the war remained hopeless, the Nazis stepped up their program for killing the Jews. The authorities sent German Jews to ghettos and annihilation camps in Poland, where many were immediately gassed. Those who were spared for slave labor knew that any moment could be their last.

In 1944, teenager Cecilia Landau was deported from Germany to the Auschwitz death camp in Poland. There, she faced the awful horrors of selections in which SS officers chose who would live and who would die:

> One evening, shortly after our arrival, Maja [the prisoner in charge of the barracks] announced that . . . Dr. Mengele would inspect the prisoners. "The procedure is simple," she said. "You take off your dress, carry it in the left hand, and walk naked past the SS inspection team. Be fast and don't talk. They'll decide."
>
> "Decide what?" I whispered to Elli [a friend].
>
> "I've heard rumors that Mengele selects some for work, some for hospital experiments, and some for the

From left to right, Josef Mengele, Rudolf Höss, Josef Kramer, and an unidentified Nazi officer. Mengele was known as the Angel of Death for his inhumane experiments at Auschwitz.

gas chambers," Elli whispered in response. Once again, the SS would determine life and death. . . .

Morning broke, gray and dismal, and again we lined up, Elli and I still together. We stood and waited, our scantily clad bodies shivering. Three SS officers suddenly marched into the center of the [compound] . . .

"The one with the baton is Mengele," someone whispered. "He is God here. He'll sentence us—to work, to the gas chambers, or the hospital."

Maja now faced us. "Achtung! Remove dresses! Carry them in your left hand. First row, march—fast! Don't dally!"

Those in front of us almost ran past the three SS officers, while Mengele appraised them like cattle, motioning—right, left, right, left.

His face was expressionless, almost casual.

"Next row!"

Elli nudged me, whispering, "Walk fast. Don't look at anyone."

Shamefully, I began running naked across the field, forcing myself not to think. Dress in hand, I stumbled past the Germans, who stood no more than three feet away. I raced on, avoiding their stares, but out of the corner of my eye I saw the swinging baton in Mengele's hand motion me to the right. Was right better than left? Elli followed close behind and was also signaled to the right. Realizing that we were still together, we breathed a sigh of relief. At least half of the group has been directed to the left and were already being led away. We soon lost sight of them.[1]

Liberating the Survivors

The people on the left most likely went straight to the gas chambers. The very old, the very young, and the obviously

Survivors of Auschwitz leave the camp after its liberation at the end of World War II. The sign above the gate, "Arbeit Macht Frei," is translated as "Work Makes You Free."

sick or crippled were usually selected for immediate death. Those who looked like they could work might be saved for a time. As the German army crumbled before the Allied advance, the trains kept running and the death camps kept killing. However, troops from the United States, Great Britain, and the Soviet Union (known in World War II as the Allies) began liberating concentration camps one by one. Many inmates were too sick for help; they died with freedom at hand. The survivors were both stunned and puzzled by this sudden liberty.

At the Woebbelin camp in Germany, teenager George Salton barely realized what was happening:

[As] I came onto that place I noticed many prisoners yelling and screaming and jumping and dancing. And there standing amongst them were seven giants, young people. They must have been 18 or 19 . . . American soldiers. There were seven or eight of them standing inside the camp. Apparently they cut the wire and came into the camp. They were bewildered by us. Wild and unkempt and dirty and, I'm sure, smelly people, jumping and dancing and trying to embrace them and kiss them. And I did too. I also joined the crowd and yelled and screamed and somehow knew that the day of liberation [had] come. It was a strange feeling for me, however, because as I remember it . . . I was overwhelmed by this unexpected and unhoped for encounter of freedom, but at the same time, what was happening was outside of me. I really . . . I didn't know what to make of it. I knew I was free, but I didn't count on it. I somehow didn't know what it meant. And I knew it was great, but . . . I was overjoyed because all people around me were overjoyed and were singing and dancing . . . [but] I was 17 . . . I was free, but what it meant I wasn't sure.[2]

Nobody in Hitler's Germany escaped unchanged after twelve years of Nazi rule. Jews and other "non-Aryans" carried nightmarish memories that would be with them for the rest of their lives. For Jewish young people, those memories included a childhood forever shattered by hatred and the knowledge that lost innocence could never be reclaimed.

Timeline

January 30, 1933—Adolf Hitler becomes chancellor of Germany.

April 25, 1933—Law Against the Crowding of German Schools and Institutions of Higher Learning restricts the number of Jewish students allowed to attend.

May 10, 1933—More than twenty thousand "un-German" books are burned in Munich.

August 2, 1934—President Paul von Hindenburg dies; Adolf Hitler declares himself both president and chancellor of Germany.

September 15, 1935—The Nuremberg Laws deprive Jews of German citizenship.

November 7, 1938—Herschel Grynszpan shoots a German Embassy official in Paris.

November 9–10, 1938—Kristallnacht, nationwide violence against Jews in Germany, follows the death of the embassy official.

November 15, 1938—Jewish students are formally expelled from German schools. They must attend only Jewish schools.

December 2–3, 1938—Jews are banned from streets on certain days and denied driver's licenses and car registrations.

December 3, 1938—Jewish teachers and students are banned from German universities.

March 22, 1941—Gypsy and African-German students are banned from German schools.

June 1942—The German government closes all Jewish schools.

April 30, 1945—Adolf Hitler commits suicide.

May 7, 1945—Germany surrenders, ending World War II in Europe.

Chapter Notes

Introduction

1. Gerald Schwab, *The Day the Holocaust Began: The Odyssey of Herschel Grynszpan* (Westport, CT: Praeger Publishers, 1990), p. 2.
2. "Kristallnacht," The History Place: World War II in Europe, 1996, http://www.historyplace.com/worldwar2/timeline/knacht.htm.

Chapter 1
Institutional Anti-Semitism

1. Dennis Showalter and William J. Astore, *Hindenburg: Icon of German Militarism* (Washington, DC: Potomac Books, 2005), p. 92.
2. Melita Maschmann, *Account Rendered: A Dossier on My Former Self* (London, UK: Abelard-Schumann, 1965), pp. 11–12.
3. Ezra BenGershôm, *David: Testimony of a Holocaust Survivor* (Oxford, UK: Berg Publishers Limited, 1988), pp. 22–23.
4. Hans J. Massaquoi, *Destined to Witness: Growing Up Black in Nazi Germany* (New York, NY: William Morrow and Company, 1999), pp. 43–45.
5. Willy Schumann, *Being Present: Growing Up in Hitler's Germany* (Kent, OH: Kent State University Press, 1991), p. 27.
6. Elizabeth Kaufmann Koenig, United States Holocaust Memorial Museum (USHMM) Oral History Interview, RG-50.030*111.
7. Edith Gerda Reimer, USHMM Survivor Testimonies, RG-01.036.
8. Lore Metzger, USHMM Archives, RG-02.018.
9. Carola Stern Steinhardt, USHMM Survivor Testimonies, RG-50.030*0368.
10. Interview with Walter F., San Francisco: Holocaust Oral History Project, May 15, 1990, http://remember.org/witness/wit.sur.franck.html.
11. Alfred Feldman, *One Step Ahead: A Jewish Fugitive in Hitler's Europe* (Carbondale, IL: Southern Illinois University Press, 2001), pp. 4–5.

Chapter 2
Jews Become Targets

1. "The Reich Citizenship Law of September 15, 1935, and the First Regulation to the Reich Citizenship Law of November 14, 1935," United States Chief Counsel for the Prosecution of Axis Criminality,

Nazi Conspiracy and Aggression, Volume IV (Washington, DC: United States Government Printing Office, 1946), Documents 1416-PS and 1417-PS, pp. 7–10.

2. Dora Kramen Dimitro, USHMM Oral History Interview, RG 50.030-0372.

3. Henry Landman, USHMM Survivors Testimonies, Archives 1997.A.0175.

4. "Regulation Requiring Jews to Change Their Names, August 1938," Yad Vashem: The Holocaust Martyrs' and Heroes' Remembrance Authority, 2004, http://www.yadvashem.org/odot_pdf/Microsoft%20Word%20-%205314.pdf.

5. Interview of Guy Stern, USHMM, RG-50.030*-223.

6. Eve Nussbaum Soumerai, *A Voice from the Holocaust* (Westport, CT: Greenwood Press, 2003), pp. 43–44.

7. Edith Gerder Reimer, USHMM Survivor Testimonies, Autobiography, RG-01.036.

8. Magda Lipner, USHMM Survivor Testimonies, RG-02.205.

9. Ernest Günter Fontheim, "A Personal Memoir of 'Kristallnacht,'" *Aufbau*, No. 26, December 18, 1998, haGalil.com, 1995–2006, http://www.hagalil.com/deutschland/berlin/gemeinde/fontheim.htm.

10. Fred Ederer, USHMM Survivor Testimonies, RG-01.087.

11. Soumerai, p. 15.

12. Ibid., pp. 36–37.

13. Ibid., pp. 49–50.

Chapter 3
The Nazification of Schools

1. "Hitler Youth," The History Place, http://www.historyplace.com/worldwar2/hitleryouth/hj-timeline.htm.

2. Henry Landman, USHMM Survivors Testimonies, Archives 1997.A.0175.

3. Simone Arnold Liebster, *Facing the Lion: Memoirs of a Young Girl in Nazi Europe* (New Orleans, LA: Grammaton Press, 2000), p. 223.

4. Interview with Survivor Walter F., San Francisco: Holocaust Oral History Project, May 15, 1990, http://remember.org/witness/wit.sur.franck.html.

5. James W. Miller, "Youth in Dictatorships," *American Political Science Review*, vol. 32, no. 5, October 1938, p. 966.

6. Hans J. Massaquoi, *Destined to Witness: Growing Up Black in Hitler's Germany* (New York, NY: William Morrow and Company, 1999), p. xii.

7. Henry Landman, USHMM Survivors Testimonies, Archives 1997.A.0175.
8. Elvira Bauer, *Trust No Fox in the Green Meadow and No Jew on His Oath* (Nuremburg, Germany: Stürmer Publishing House, 1936), English translation by Edward J. Kunzer, "The Youth of Nazi Germany," *Journal of Educational Sociology*, Vol. 11, No. 6, February 1938, p. 348.
9. Ezra BenGershôm, *David: Testimony of a Holocaust Survivor* (Oxford, UK: Berg Publishers Limited, 1988), p. 43.
10. Masssaquoi, pp. 67–68.
11. Interview with survivor Walter F., May 15, 1990.
12. Lore Metzger, USHMM Archives, RG 02.018.
13. Klaus Langer, "Diary Entry November 16, 1938," in Alexandra Zapruder, ed., *Salvaged Pages: Young Writers' Diaries of the Holocaust* (New Haven, CT: Yale University Press, 2002).

Chapter 4
Gentiles Trapped within the System

1. "The Hitler Youth," The History Place, http://www.historyplace.com/worldwar2/hitleryouth/index.html.
2. Willy Schumann, *Being Present: Growing Up in Hitler's Germany* (Kent, OH: Kent State University Press, 1991), p. 40.
3. Ibid., pp. 41–43.
4. Ibid., p. 29.
5. Melita Maschmann, *Account Rendered: A Dossier on My Former Self* (London, UK: Abelard-Schumann, 1965), pp. 40–41.
6. Jurgen Herbst, *Requiem for a German Past: A Boyhood Among the Nazis* (Madison, WI: University of Wisconsin Press, 1999), pp. 73–74.
7. Ibid., pp. 64–65.
8. United States Holocaust Memorial Museum. "Nazi Persecution of Jehovah's Witnesses." Holocaust Encyclopedia, www.ushmm.org/wlc/en/article.php?ModuleId=10005394.
9. Simone Arnold Liebster, Facing the Lion: Memoirs of a Young Girl in Nazi Europe (New Orleans, LA: Grammaton Press, 2000), pp. 179–81.
10. "Last Letter from Wolfgang Kusserow," Kusserow Family Collection, USHMM RG-32.002*01.
11. Irmgard A. Hunt, *On Hitler's Mountain: Overcoming the Legacy of a Nazi Childhood* (New York, NY: Harper Perennial, 2006), p. 155–158.
12. Alfons Heck, *The Burden of Hitler's Legacy* (Phoenix, AZ: Renaissance House Publishers, 1988), pp. 106–107.
13. "Mentally and Physically Handicapped: Victims of the Nazi Era," United States Holocaust Memorial Museum, https://www.ushmm.org/

learn/students/learning-materials-and-resources/mentally-and-physically-handicapped-victims-of-the-nazi-era.

14. Hunt, pp. 66–67.

15. Ibid., pp. 68–70.

Chapter 5
Nazi Youth Organizations

1. "Hitler Youth: Principles and Ideology," Historical Boys' Uniforms, November 4, 2002, http://histclo.com/youth/youth/org/nat/hitler/prin/hj-prin.htm.

2. Alfons Heck, Child of Hitler: Germany in the Days When God Wore a Swastika (Phoenix, AZ: Renaissance House Publishers, 1985), p. 9.

3. Ibid., pp. 1–3.

4. J. Noaakes and G. Pridham, eds., *Nazism: A History in Documents and Eyewitness Accounts, 1919–1945*, Vol. 1 (New York, NY: Schocken Books, 1983), pp. 480–481.

5. Jurgen Herbst, *Requiem for a German Past: A Boyhood Among the Nazis* (Madison, WI: University of Wisconsin Press, 1999), p. 91.

6. Irmgard A. Hunt, *On Hitler's Mountain: Overcoming the Legacy of a Nazi Childhood* (New York, NY: Harper Perennial, 2006), pp. 171–174.

7. Carola Stern Steinhardt, USHMM Survivor Testimonies, RG-50.030*0368.

8. Hans J. Massaquoi, *Destined to Witness: Growing Up Black in Hitler's Germany* (New York, NY: William Morrow and Company, 1999), pp. 99–100.

9. "German Swing Youth," Swingstyle Syndicate, http://www.return2style.de/amiswhei.htm.

10. "German Resistance to Hitler: Walter Meyer," United States Holocaust Memorial Museum, Collections, https://www.ushmm.org/wlc/en/media_oi.php?ModuleId=0&MediaId=1236.

11. Detler J.K. Reukert, *Inside Germany: Conformity, Opposition, and Racism in Everyday Life* (New Haven, CT: Yale University Press, 1987), pp. 157–158.

12. "White Rose—Leaflet 5," libcom.org, December 6, 2005, http://libcom.org/library/white-rose-leaflet-5.

13. "Hitler's Boy Soldiers: 1939–1945," The History Place, 1999, http://www.historyplace.com/worldwar2/hitleryouth/hj-boy-soldiers.htm.

14. Gerhardt B. Thamm, *Boy Soldier: A German Teenager at the Nazi Twilight* (Jefferson, NC: McFarland & Company, 1999), p. 2.
15. Ibid., p. 108.
16. "Hitler's Boy Soldiers: 1939–1945."
17. Ibid.

Chapter 6
The "Final Solution" and the End of the War

1. Lucille Eichengreen, *From Ashes to Life: My Memories of the Holocaust* (San Francisco, CA: Mercury House, 1994), pp. 99–100.
2. "George Salton Describes Liberation by American Soldiers," United States Holocaust Memorial Museum, Liberation of Nazi Camps,https://www.ushmm.org/wlc/en/media_oi.php?ModuleId=0&MediaId=3279.

Glossary

Aryan Hitler's name for the Germanic and Nordic "master race."

chancellor Head of government in a parliamentary system who carries out the business of government and supervises its various agencies.

concentration camp A camp for confining political prisoners, enemy aliens, and civilians who ran afoul of the government.

crematorium Large, super-hot furnace for burning bodies.

dissident Someone who actively opposes the state.

final solution The term for the Nazi plan to solve what they called the "Jewish problem" or "Jewish question" by killing all the Jews in Europe.

gas chamber In Nazi Germany, a sealed room for killing groups of people; often disguised as a shower room.

Gestapo (Geheimestaatspolizei) Internal security police known for terrorist methods against persons suspected of treason or disloyalty to Nazi Germany.

ghetto In Nazi Germany, a rundown area in a city or town where Jews were confined.

indoctrinate To teach an uncritical acceptance of a particular point of view.

ostracize To exclude a person or group of people from a society.

prohibit To disallow or make illegal.

propaganda A one-sided communication, presenting a single point of view.

Reichstag German parliament; also, the parliament building.

storm troopers Members of the militarized branch of the Nazi Party; also know as brownshirts.

visa Travel papers allowing a person to enter a country.

Further Reading

Books

Bornstein, Michael, and Debbie Bornstein Holinstat. *Survivors Club: The True Story of a Very Young Prisoner of Auschwitz*. New York, NY: Farrar, Straus & Giroux, 2017.

Deem, James M. *The Prisoners of Breendonk: Personal Histories from a World War II Concentration Camp*. New York, NY: HMH Books for Young Readers, 2015

Frankl, Viktor. *Man's Search for Meaning: Young Adult Edition*. New York, NY: Beacon Press, 2017.

Gruenbaum, Michael. *Somewhere There Is Still a Sun: A Memoir of the Holocaust*. New York, NY: Aladdin, 2015.

Shackleton, Kath. *Survivors of the Holocaust*. London, UK: Hachette, 2016.

Yolen, Jane. *Mapping the Bones*. New York, NY: Philomel Books, 2018.

Websites

BBC—The Holocaust Year by Year
www.bbc.co.uk/timelines/z86nfg8
An interactive timeline displaying the events of each year of the Holocaust.

History Channel Online
www.history.com/topics/world-war-ii/the-holocaust
The online branch of the History Channel offers videos and articles about the Holocaust more generally.

How Stuff Works: Stuff You Missed in History Class
www.missedinhistory.com/tags/world-war-ii.htm
A plethora of podcasts on all aspects of World War II.

The United States Holocaust Memorial Museum
www.ushmm.org/learn/students/the-holocaust-a-learning-site-for-students
The museum, located in Washington, DC, has a vast online archive of survivor interviews, informational articles, videos, and images.

Films

Defiance, dir. Edward Zwick, 2008.

"Escape from Auschwitz," April 29, 2008, *Secrets of the Dead: Unearthing History*, PBS, television program.

Index